SASKATCHEWAN

Book of *Musts*

The 101 Places Every Saskatchewanian MUST See

If you think you know Saskatchewan, think again

D. Grant Black

TO OUR READERS

Every effort has been made by the author and the editor to ensure that the information in this book is accurate and up-to-date. We revise and update annually yet details can change after a book is published. If you discover any out-of-date or incorrect information in the *Saskatchewan Book of Musts*, we'd appreciate hearing about it via our website: **bookofeverything.com**

MacIntyre Purcell Publishing Inc.
232 Lincoln St., PO Box 1142
Lunenburg, Nova Scotia
B0J 2C0 Canada

www.bookofeverything.com
info@bookofeverything.com

Cover photo courtesy: Dave Reede Photography
Author photo: Patricia Dawn Robertson
Full-page photos: iStock
Small photos provided by the individuals and/or organizations featured in the book.
Printed and bound in Canada by Friesens.

Library and Archives Canada Cataloguing in Publication

Black, D. Grant
    Saskatchewan Book of Musts / D. Grant Black

ISBN 978-0-9810941-3-7

    1. Saskatchewan--Guidebooks. I. Title.

FC3507.B53 2009   917.12404'4   C2009-904603-2

Introduction

Saskatchewanians are unpretentious by nature. Maybe our strategy is, "why brag about our good fortune in case the rest of Canada hears about it and wants to move here?" We certainly don't want to promote the fact that we can drive across people-friendly cities like Regina or Saskatoon in a mere 15 minutes or that sparkling lakes are within easy reach.

Saskatchewan, the Prairies' middle child, is possibly better known for producing bushels of grain and populist politicians than as a tourist mecca. Yet with a population of just over a million in a province roughly twice the size of Germany, there's an expansive landscape to explore, vibrant urban areas and a rich cultural history.

For a so-called "flat and boring" province, humble Saskatchewan boasts a diverse range of terrain and ecosystems. Just witness the Athabasca Sand Dunes Wilderness Park in the north, Grassland National Park's wild Prairie in the south, or the anomalous alpine of the Cypress Hills in the west (the highest point of land in southern Canada between the Rockies and Labrador).

Our 1,000-plus northern lakes are surrounded by boreal forest and Precambrian Shield rock and the entire province is a major migratory route for dozens of North American bird species, including pelicans.

We're Canada's sunniest province and solar-powered Saskatchewanians revel in an average of 260 annual days of sunshine. Of course, it could be either plus or minus 40 at the time, but it's still sunshine. Whether in your backyard or gathered around a campfire, the Northern lights and stargazing are our outdoors evening show, with free admission and not a bad seat anywhere.

I've compiled a mere slice of our province's often quirky topographical, historical and cultural locations — along with just some of our finest farm to fork cuisine. Fourteen dynamic Saskatchewanians also graciously contributed their own Must lists.

I'd like to thank my partner in life and in word farming, writer Patricia Dawn Robertson, who put up with my long disappearances in front of the computer, or when I committed the ultimate home office *faux pas*: talking about this book in the kitchen.

Thanks also to Daryl Demoskoff at Tourism Saskatchewan, and, of course, John MacIntyre, Kelly Inglis and Tim Lehnert at MacIntyre Purcell Publishing Inc.

Enjoy this handy book of 101 Saskatchewan Musts, your new guide to our land of living skies.

— D. Grant Black, October 2009

TABLE OF CONTENTS

Regina

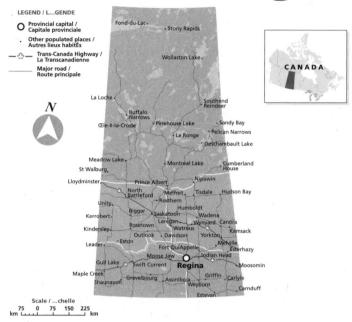

LEGEND / LÉGENDE

○ Provincial capital /
　Capitale provinciale

· Other populated places /
　Autres lieux habités

—◇— Trans-Canada Highway /
　La Transcanadienne

—— Major road /
　Route principale

N

CANADA

Scale / échelle
75　0　75　150　225
km ┗┴┴┴┴┘ km

Piffles' Playground		**1**

If you've never been to a Saskatchewan Roughriders game, then either you're not a football fan or you've just arrived in Saskatchewan and haven't been converted to the unofficial provincial religion yet.

From June to November, it's football season. To participate in a Mosaic Stadium at Taylor Field home game, rabid fans, swathed in green, drive from every corner of the province to show their "Rider Pride" (a term coined in 1979 by the irascible sportswriter John Robertson when he helped save the Riders from extinction).

During the summer, hardcore fans consume the contents of a watermelon then create two jaunty helmets with a permanent marker "S" on the side. In October, these same strident fans, usually unadvisedly shirtless and painted green, don green pumpkin helmets to show their varsity allegiance. No wonder we have the reputation of the CFL's greatest fans.

The Saskatchewan Roughriders' home field dates back to 1912 when it was just a simple rugby field. Located at the current Mosaic Stadium site, the first Rider teams played on Park Hughes' field where families would circle the rugby field to watch the games.

Since the Riders' founding, Neil "Piffles" Taylor had been instrumental in the early development of the Roughriders as a player, coach and executive. When he died suddenly in 1946 at the age of 48, the City of Regina renamed the Riders' home Taylor Field in 1947 as a salute to this great man.

In 1948, a $47,000 investment was made to build a 4,500-seat grandstand on the west side of the playing area and in the mid-1970s a major renovation included the addition of a second level to the west-side grandstand, new offices, dressing room facilities — and the first artificial turf.

Until the SaskTel MaxTron video board was unveiled in time for the 2005 season, most of us didn't dare take our eyes off the field or risk missing a key play. Like a giant step into the CFL big leagues, Roughrider fans could now watch replays like other clubs.

Almost 60 years after the field was named for Piffles Taylor, the football club, in conjunction with the City of Regina, re-branded Taylor Field in 2006 as "Mosaic Stadium at Taylor Field."

Until 2016, Mosaic, the corporate potash giant, will be the new stamp on the beloved Taylor Field where legends like Ron Lancaster and George Reed once racked up points on the board like a couple of seasoned cribbage masters.

To commemorate the great man in perpetuity, a reconstructed monument now stands at the entrance and the street in front of the stadium been permanently re-named "Piffles Taylor Way."

After a Riders game, be sure to stop for ice cream at the Milky Way (910 Victoria Ave.). This Regina landmark is only open in summer and their pistachio soft ice cream kicks butt like the Riders with home field advantage.

Details: *Check out the season game schedule for those increasingly elusive home game tickets, 1-888-4-RIDERS (1-888-474-3377), saskriders.com*

TAKE 5 THOMAS & DEBORAH RUSH
FOODIES' FIVE STELLAR URBAN NOSHERIES

Thomas, a Red Seal-certified chef, and his wife, Deborah, a Saskatchewan-raised marketing-publicity consultant, live in Regina with son Dylan, daughter Taylor and their Bernese mountain dog, Sadie. This foodie couple pursue their passion for fine dining through regular visits to Saskatchewan's vibrant urban restaurants.

1. **crave kitchen + wine bar in Regina**. Located in the former home of the Assiniboia Club, this Victoria Avenue hotspot caters to groups from four to 120 people with excellent food and wine selections. A Friday business lunch should include a steak sandwich with succulent aged beef and frites cooked to perfection. After work drinks are equally exceptional; crave has the most extensive tequila selection ever!

2. **La Bodega in Regina**. La Bodega marries the art of tapas with an extensive wine list and through solid kitchen preparation, this mainstay on South Albert Street shines like a jewel in restaurateur Adam Sperling's food crown. The private room with its original fireplace is perfect for all gatherings and, if you're in Regina during a Saskatchewan winter, the award-winning ice bar (made of ice!) is the perfect antidote for the most jaded business traveller.

3. **The Willows on Wascana in Regina**. This perennial favourite overlooking Wascana Lake has it all: five-star food, winning wines and exemplary service, all surrounded by the most beautiful view in the province. Chef-owner Moe Mathieu continues to dazzle with homegrown delicacies and the knowledgeable staff can add a wine flight (specialized tasting) that will take the most mundane dinner to new heights.

4. **2nd Ave Grill in Saskatoon**. The real star of this outstanding downtown grill is the wine list. The most discriminate oenophile will find a pleasing vintage, both specialty and rare finds that make a good dinner great. Coupled with their delicious duck breast, you have a winning combination.

5. **Bliss Fine Food in Saskatoon**. Bliss, the newest kid in the Broadway District, may not be as pretty as the others, but the food shines, with a varied menu and a few surprises. Bliss puts a nice spin on some traditional favourites — vanilla fennel slaw and bacon corn relish — and the fresh and interesting salads provide a nice alternative to the overworked Caesar.

Some mornings you just don't want to cook breakfast. That's where seasoned Regina restauranteurs like Nick Makris and his brother, John (owner of the Diplomat Steakhouse), who arrived in 1965 from Greece, come into the culinary picture.

If you live in the Queen City, you probably already know about Nicky's Café and Bake Shop. If you're visiting, definitely start your day with breakfast at Nicky's.

Housed east of the humble warehouse district at 8th Ave. and Winnipeg St., this out-of-the-way café serves the best breakfast in the city. Nicky's is the spot where early morning diners can scarf down scrumptious fennel sausages and eggs to fill up for a day of navigating Regina.

Co-owner Nick Makris has been coming out of the kitchen in his white apron to kibitz with his loyal customers for over 20 years. There's a reason why they come back: Nicky's serves a full plate of wholesome food for a reasonable price plus the place makes you feel like a regular, even if it's your first time.

Nicky's is especially the place to see and be seen on a weekend morning in Regina. Watch for the affable Mayor Pat Fiacco, an ex-boxer who eats and networks at the popular eatery, usually still in his workout clothes.

Nicky's is like one of those classic diners from the past when food used to taste like it was cooked at home by your mother — only better. This busy spot also serves lunch where Nicky's chefs create additive-free burgers, roast their own beef, slice their own bacon and prepare every dish fresh. Nick even claims that you won't find a can-opener in the kitchen of Nicky's Café.

Home-made soups, like Nicky's famous lentil soup that originated 15 years ago, contains lentils right from a local seed plant. Many full meals are under $10. They even cater.

At Nicky's, you feel like you've joined a large, extended Greek family. Before you're out the door, Nick will make sure you take home a freshly baked loaf of his flax bread. Who wouldn't?

Details: *Nicky's can get pretty busy on a weekend morning or any mealtime, so be prepared to wait in line while your stomach grumbles and the scent of other diners' meals waft by. Open 5:30 am – 9:00 pm, 1005–8th Ave., (306) 757-3222*

Day at the Museum | 3

When I was a pre-schooler, my sizeable family and I visited Regina in the summertime. I can prove it with actual 8 mm colour film stock of my Depression-era mother feeding us yet another picnic lunch in front of the Royal Saskatchewan Museum. It's that boxy Tyndall stone building on Albert Street South with the very long sidewalk, adjacent gardens and a huge lawn like an English estate.

After filling up on bologna and Miracle Whip sandwiches, wilted carrot sticks and warm water out of a wax-paper-sealed Miracle Whip jar, our family museum visit was a wonder to behold for a Prairie kid: elaborate exhibits of natural and human history and all that glossy slab marble. I was hooked.

Formed in 1906, this was the first museum in Saskatchewan and the first provincial museum in the Prairie provinces with an aim to "secure and preserve natural history specimens and objects of historical and ethnological interest." The government even set aside $557.70 (approximately $10,000 today) to purchase "Natural History Specimens."

The new museum, initially under the jurisdiction of the Department of Agriculture, originally lacked a clear collections policy yet it still acquired an interesting variety of objects: postage stamps of the world collection, an old horseshoe, Hindu embroidery, Zulu necklaces, a girdle and shield, Mesopotamia greeting cards, Mexican feather work, a Jamaican hat, a U.S. three-cent bill, *A History of Scotland* (vol. 1), one polar bear foot and a boot worn by Captain Scott during his South Pole expedition.

Almost 100 years later, the museum's collection and three galleries are substantially more focused and hi-tech.

Visitors to the Earth Sciences Gallery discover how it took over three billion years to create the earth. The Life Sciences Gallery takes a close look at both Saskatchewan's plants, animals and landscapes in different seasons and the First Nations Gallery features items from the museum's collections plus life-size and miniature dioramas that depict Native people's history.

Kids are greeted with a throaty roar at the museum's theatre by a half-sized robotic Tyrannosaurus rex affectionately named "Megamunch" and regular kid-centred events at the Megamunch Club (kids 5–8), such as "Beetlemania," is where youngsters learn just how many kinds of beetles reside in Saskatchewan.

Details: *The Royal Saskatchewan Museum is located at 2445 Albert Street South (at College Ave.). Open year-round except Christmas Day. Admission by donation. (306) 787-2815 or 787-2816, royalsaskmuseum.ca*

4 | The Hotel

Once, before the generic elegance of modern luxury hotels, there was the majestic spawn of Canada's two great continental railways. The railway age heralded a new era in hotels. The Chateau Frontenac, built in 1892 by the Canadian Pacific Railway in Québec City, started a tradition of railway hotels that became a distinctively Canadian architectural art form.

By the mid-1920s, CPR officials decided it was time that the "Queen City of the Western Plains" needed a grand hotel to add to their far-flung chain of Canadian hotels. They chose the site of E.N. Darke's first residence on Victoria Avenue, across from Victoria Park, to build Regina's first and only railway hotel.

Regina's railway hotel was built in only 11 months. During the peak of construction, 1,000 labourers and tradesmen worked in shifts of 24 hours to complete the hotel, often in frigid winter temperatures.

The materials were shipped by rail from around Canada. One of the most obvious architectural features in this modernist classical structure was that favourite facade also found on the Royal Saskatchewan Museum, the Legislature and many other 20th century buildings around the province: pale, Manitoba Tyndall stone.

The hotel's interior was the epitome of luxury. This 10-storey structure, the second highest building in Regina at the time after the

TAKE 5 SHEILA COLES
FIVE SASKATCHEWAN STAYCATIONS

Sheila Coles, host of CBC Radio One's *The Morning Edition*, was born in England, but the Brits packed off her to the colonies before she reached the ripe old age of three. She then spent the next 20 years looking for a place that would let her stay. Stops along the way included Winnipeg, Vancouver, Edmonton, St. John's, Beijing, Barbados and Jersey, Channel Islands. Saskatchewan said no, but she stayed anyway, agreeing to do her bit to keep the population up (three kids: Lisa, Alison and Nathan). Sheila feels she has the best job in journalism and hopes the powers-that-be will continue to let her call Saskatchewan home. Sheila lives in Regina's Cathedral district with the above-mentioned offspring, her long-suffering husband and her adorable epileptic Labrador retriever, Oskar.

1. **Go for a run around Regina's beautiful Wascana Lake.** You'll see the legislative building, a marina, and, if you're lucky, kayak and canoe racing. Watch out for the geese, though. They — and their "leavings" — are everywhere!

2. **Have a latte or a delicious "Samurai Bowl" on the patio of 13th Avenue Coffee House in Regina**. Then go for a stroll along 13th Avenue. Make sure you stop into Traditions Handcraft Gallery to pick up a beautiful Saskatchewan craft. We have the best potters in the country. One weekend in May, the avenue is closed off for a fabulous street fair, part of the Cathedral Village Arts Festival.

3. **You can't miss taking a walk by the South Saskatchewan River in Saskatoon**. For a panoramic view, take the railway bridge from one side to the other.

4. **Broadway Avenue in Saskatoon is the place to find wonderful local shops and bistros**. For a carbo-licious treat, have a burger at the Broadway Cafe. If it's earlier in the day, the breakfasts are scrumptious, too. And, if there's something good on, catch a show at the Broadway Theatre across the street.

5. **Book a canoe trip on one of hundreds of pristine northern lakes or rivers.** Ric at Churchill River Canoe Outfitters will help you. But shhhh ... don't tell anyone else. The beauty of our north is one of our best-kept secrets!

Legislative Building, was self-contained with its own power and water source. The foyer featured vaulted, decorated ceilings and marble thresholds. This luxurious inn also contained the most sophisticated kitchen in the city, which included an automated vegetable peeler.

Built at a cost of $1.2 million, the Hotel Saskatchewan opened on May 24, 1927, just a few convenient blocks from CPR's passenger line. Regina now had its grand palace to accommodate and entertain the upper classes, especially visiting royalty. It was the hub of the city's social life. To Reginans, it was endearingly known as "The Hotel." As befit its stature, the Hotel Saskatchewan even housed several Lieutenant-Governors from 1945–1984.

By the late 1980s, after changing ownership a few times, the hotel ran into receivership problems due to costly renovations and lost revenue. After new ownership that saw a two-year restoration program return the Hotel Saskatchewan to its original grandeur, Radisson Hotels franchised the now 224-room hotel in 1992. By 1993, Regina City Council recognized the value of this Queen City jewel and designated the Hotel Saskatchewan a municipal heritage site.

While royalty such as Queen Elizabeth II have stayed in the decadent Royal Suite several times over the years, some of the UK's less desirable citizens have also darkened the Hotel Saskatchewan's doorway. In 2006, rock 'n roll's royalty, the Rolling Stones — who played two sold-out concerts at Mosaic Stadium — took over most of the hotel.

Some hotels will let anybody in. Go see it for yourself.

Details: *The Radisson Plaza Hotel Saskatchewan is located at 2125 Victoria Avenue in the Queen City's downtown core. (306) 522-7691, hotelsask.com*

Haight-Ashbury with Tilley Hats | 5

After enduring another long harsh winter, no one relishes the short summer like feisty Prairie people. That's why the Regina Folk Festival, Western Canada's longest-running festival of music, art and culture, is still a favourite Saskatchewan summer event.

Since 1969, for one brief weekend each August, scenic Victoria Park in downtown Regina morphs into Haight-Ashbury with Tilley hats. The normally sedate populace dons a favourite tie-dye folkie outfit and lets loose to the eclectic mix of musical styles: Americana country, bluegrass, operatic rock, world, singer-songwriters, roots and blues, Celtic, funk, reggae, jazz and even spoken word.

Since only about 15,000 people descend on the park over the weekend, this makes the festival feel more like a very big house party than a public event. Folkies get a chance to dine on local curry, buy handmade earrings in the Arts Markets, and take the kids to the nearby Children's area — all within a short walk from the main stage.

Stellar line-ups in recent years have included that manic power-house act from San Francisco, Michael Franti and Spearhead, rocking the house on a Saturday night to established Canadian acts like Blue Rodeo, Kathleen Edwards, Broken Social Scene, The Weakerthans, The Great Lake Swimmers, Bedouin Soundclash, Corb Lund and Saskatchewan's own The Deep Dark Woods.

While we wait for another Folk Fest, the organizers operate the concert series during the rest of the year with soulful touring acts like Martin Sexton and Alex Cuba at various local venues.

Details: *The Regina Folk Festival runs annually for three days (Fri. to Sun.) in the first week of August. An adult Early Bird Weekend Pass sells for $75 (to June 30). Check for dates, other ticket prices and this year's performers: 1-866-954-5623, reginafolkfestival.com*

6   The Lawyer's Gift

Long before Saskatoon's Fred Mendel there was Regina's Norman MacKenzie. MacKenzie was a prominent Regina lawyer and dedicated patron of the arts. From 1911 until his death in 1936, he assembled Saskatchewan's first art collection of note.

The MacKenzie Art Gallery in Regina's T.C. Douglas Building is the legacy of Norman MacKenzie. But it's only been located there since 1990.

MacKenzie actually provided the impetus for the gallery when he bequeathed his collection, along with an endowment, to the University of Saskatchewan, Regina College. The Norman MacKenzie Art Gallery opened in 1953 as a university-run gallery at the Regina Campus of the University of Saskatchewan (later the University of Regina).

The MacKenzie soon developed a national reputation for its contemporary exhibitions. When the MacKenzie hived off from the University of Regina in 1990, it became the community-based MacKenzie Art Gallery in a new and expanded facility within the T.C. Douglas Building on Albert Street South. Over 160,000 art enthusiasts now visit the MacKenzie annually.

This 31,000-square-metre space is spread out on three levels. The exhibition level alone — eight environmentally controlled galleries

— encompasses 7,300 square metres.

Visitors will find a permanent art collection from historical to contemporary Canadian, American and International artists, major touring exhibitions, programs and even a gallery shop where many of Saskatchewan's artists and craftspeople sell their work, both two-dimensional and three-dimensional creations.

Details: *The MacKenzie Gallery and Gallery Shop are open Mon. to Thurs. 10 am – 5:30 pm, Fri.: 10 am – 9 pm and Sat., Sun. and statutory holidays, 12 pm – 5:30 pm. Admission is free, but donations are welcomed. 3475 Albert Street South, Regina, (306) 584-4250, mackenzieartgallery.ca*

Queen City Oasis 7

The Queen City shows best in the summer. With 350,000 hand-planted trees greening up our capital, Regina knows how to gussy itself up for company.

You can find a large chunk of those hand-planted trees in Wascana Centre, designed in 1961 by Minoru Yamasaki, the Seattle-born architect best known as the designer of the original World Trade Center in New York.

This 1,000-hectare, 9.3-square-kilometre lakeside park and bird sanctuary is the Central Park of the Queen City. You'll find cycling and walking paths plus plenty of park benches where you can kick back and watch the Canada geese.

Politicos can take a free tour of the majestic provincial legislative building while their artsy companions can slip into the adjacent MacKenzie Art Gallery. Two founts of knowledge, the Royal Saskatchewan Museum and the Saskatchewan Science Centre, are also contained within Wascana Centre.

Two of Regina's great restaurants can be found in Wascana Centre. For lunch, look no farther than **Zest Restaurant** (306-522-5250, zestrestaurant.ca), located at the Saskatchewan Science

Centre. Co-owner and chef Rob Fuller, former personal chef to romance writer Danielle Steel, offers a tasty nouvelle cuisine menu, a weekend brunch menu on Saturdays and Sundays and gluten-free menu items for lunch and dinner. For those who want to indulge in

TAKE5 AIMEE SCHULHAUSER
A CHEF'S FIVE FAVOURITE
"MARKET TO TABLE" SOURCES

Born and raised in Cupar, Aimee Schulhauser is the owner and executive chef of evolution catering and fine foods (ecff.ca) on Lorne Street, Regina's premiere catering company. This former geologist re-trained as a chef in Calgary, learned the catering industry then moved back to Saskatchewan for the finer things in life. Aimee's self-described "boutique-style" cooking allows her to play with local ingredients on a daily basis and feature them in evolution's ever-changing menu.

1. **Zee-Bee Honey in Zehner (zeebeehoney.ca).** Michelle and Parry Frischholz's bees produce a delicious, pure unpasteurized honey. All their hives are located on organic land that gives the bees access to lots of pure sweet nectar. Zee-Bee products can be found at Regina's Farmers' Market.

2. **CharlieCrop in Regina (306) 352-0095.** I get the freshest, most beautiful basil straight from this urban greenhouse, delivered to my front door. They also carry tarragon and salad greens at various times throughout the year.

3. **Ngoy Hoa Asian Foods in Regina (306) 757-4264.** This little gem of a store on 11th Avenue supplies me with green and jasmine tea, banana leaves, spices and any kind of noodle imaginable, all at very reasonable prices. I've also purchased unique serving plates and bowls there.

4. **Body Fuel Organics in Regina (bodyfuelorganics.ca).** When I need certain hard-to-find grains or pulses, I head over to Body Fuel Organics on Ottawa Street. Owner Lana Andreasen sources organic grain flours from R & J Milling in Riceton. She also does extensive research to find an ever-changing range of products so I know that whenever I drop by, I'm sure to find another new ingredient.

5. **Grandma's Garden in Cupar.** Okay, so not everyone has access to my Grandma Eleanor's garden! Every year, we discuss what vegetables we're going to grow that season then Grandma plants them. During the harvest season, I plan my menus around what will be ready to pick that week. I'm one lucky chef and I know it! To get almost same effect without having to raid Grandma's garden, the Regina Farmers' Market (reginafarmersmarket.ca) also does the trick.

wheat and sugar, Fuller's trademark Sticky Toffee Pudding (his mum's recipe) is a rich finish to a filling lunch.

For dinner, **Willow on Wascana** (3000 Wascana Drive, 306-585-3663, willowonwascana.ca) is Regina's only resto by the lake. Since it opened its dining room in 2004, it's also one of Regina's best upscale eating experiences. The Willow on Wascana serves up a menu derived from seasonal, Saskatchewan-grown ingredients — what foodies call "micro-regional."

Chef and owner Moe Mathieu and his Willow Team take diners on a culinary tour of Saskatchewan that features ingredients from many farms around the province, all in a casual, elegant setting. Try their table hôte five-course menu and linger over wine as you enjoy a classic Prairie sunset. This is the much-needed romantic spot on the shores of Lake Wascana to rekindle the love fires.

After dinner, rent a paddleboat and enjoy the lake firsthand or take a walk over to the lookout from the top deck of the Wascana Centre Authority building.

8   The Ledge

After Roughriders football, politics is the second most popular sport in Saskatchewan. And while the Riders have their stadium, so do the politicians. They call it "the Ledge."

From September to May, the sparring between the province's 58 MLAs reverberates off the walls of this majestic edifice.

The Saskatchewan Legislative Building was designed by two Montréal architects, Edward and William Sutherland Maxwell, and built for $1.75 million between 1908-12. The Maxwells supervised the construction by P. Lyall & Sons, also a Montreal firm who later built the Centre Block of our federal Parliament Building.

This Regina landmark, which opened in October 1912, displays the beaux-arts style, an architectural movement popular in Canadian public architecture during the early 20th century. The symmetrical design of its façades, classical details and the building's interior all show the beaux-arts influence.

The Legislative Building stands out on the Prairies like any elaborate domed building you'd find around the British Commonwealth — or in the other three western provincial capital cities.

Whether inside or outside in the Legislature gardens, wedding photography is a summer mainstay of our province's political house. The Grand Staircase, Rotunda and Prince of Wales entrance are popular, approved — and free — settings for wedding parties.

When visitors walk into the Legislative building for a free tour or to digitally capture their wedding day, the Legislative Building Rotunda and Entrance to the Legislative Chamber stands out with its murals, arches and towering green marble Doric columns. You definitely know you're not standing in Mosaic Stadium.

Details: *The Saskatchewan Legislative Building is located at 2405 Legislative Drive. Free tours are available every day (except Christmas Day, New Year's Day and Good Friday) in English and French and conducted on the hour and on the half hour. Tour bookings, (306) 787-5358; wedding photography, (306) 787-5416, or find both forms online at legassembly.sk.ca*

Cathedral Village   9

Once just a middle-class enclave of 1920s sprawl dotted with two-storey houses and towering churches, Regina's Cathedral Village is now better known for its cool factor.

The "West End" shopping district is primarily centred around 13th Avenue (the Village's main corridor) — from Albert to Elphinstone streets.

Savvy shoppers and people watchers who venture into the Queen City's urban village can expect an eclectic assortment of chic goods and services: upscale clothing boutiques, salons, spas, funky contemporary and retro furnishings, eccentric gift stores and galleries, music and book shops, bistros and coffee shops, a gourmet butcher shop — even an imported fish market smack dab in the middle of the Prairies.

Here are just some of the best places to check out in Cathedral Village:

FASHION

Birthed by a pregnant entrepreneur, **Groovy Mama** is the Queen City's first maternity store and stocks mostly Canadian or locally-made products for mum and tot, from belly casting kits and prenatal workout videos to cloth diapers, toys and Robeez products.
3100 13 Ave., (306) 347-BABY (2229), groovymama.net

Indigo/Sharawaggi, an eclectic clothing and gift store in a former antique shop, houses Russian porcelain, Japanese culinary accessories, pure living organic bedding, Asian scarves plus casual wash 'n wear blouses, skirts and dresses for hot Prairie summers from Putamayo and Whitewash.
2824 13 Ave., (306) 565-2670

BEAUTY

A trip to **In Salon Spa's** terracotta-plastered walls and tile floors is the closest Reginans can get to Tuscany without taking their shoes off at the airport. This Tuscan-themed spa/salon provides hair services, aesthetics, massage, electrolysis, skin care and the newest in shape-shifting techniques, Eurowave body sculpting.

2114 Robinson St., (306) 525-6303

GIFTS

The giant circular display desk is the first thing you see in this tiny retail space. Like a Japanese curio shop, **Paper Umbrella** sells decorative and handmade papers in various textures, colours and patterns plus a selection of journals, pens, stationery, books — even chocolate-covered Saskatchewan cherries.

2724 13 Ave., (306) 522-3800, paperumbrella.ca

An artist-owned venue in a century-old building, **Mysteria** features zen-like art, hand-crafted jewellery from Regina's Melody Armstrong and Vancouver's Joanna Lovett plus fine objects from other Canadian and international artisans. In the upstairs gallery, regular exhibitions rotate between established and emerging local talent.

706 13 Ave., (306) 522-0080, mysteria.ca

FOOD & DRINK

The Crushed Grape Wine & Food Bar is the hip place to unwind in Cathedral Village. Imbibers can choose from an entire wall of premium vintages and there are more cheese varieties than a European deli. Try the signature dish, The Crushed Grape Fondue.

2118 Robinson St., (306) 352-9463, thecrushedgrape.ca

HOME

Café Orange Kitchen Toys & Tools, a former doctor's office, now dispenses gourmet coffee, desserts and full meals. High-end European kitchen utensils are on display in the café's rear from Alessi, Swissmar, Peugot, Riedel, Le Menu, Henckel, Global, Maurier and Kasumi. Gourmet food products include Lesley Stowe's crackers.

2136a Robinson St., (306) 569-0820

The eclectic **Willow Studio** offers tactile contemporary furnishings and accessories from quality Canadian manufacturers plus imported carpets and local art. Nesters can find leather and upholstered sofas, sectionals and chairs from Calgary's Whittaker Furniture and indoor/outdoor furniture from Vancouver's Ratana.

3424 13 Ave., (306) 522-9226, willowstudio.ca

10   Mountie Museum

According to a 1996 research study, the Canadian Mountie, dressed in red serge jacket, Stetson hat and Strathcona boots is — after Coca-Cola — the second most widely recognized visual icon in the world.

Imagine that familiar RCMP brand housed in a dynamic 21,000-square-metre facility on the same grounds as where Mounties are born.

Opened in May 2007, the RCMP Heritage Centre on Regina's Dewdney Avenue is the newest addition to the Heritage Corridor that features late 19th century historical structures: the Northwest Territorial Building, the RCMP Forensic Laboratory, the original head-quarters of the Northwest Mounted Police and Government House, residence of Saskatchewan's Lieutenant-Governor.

The Arthur Erickson/P3 Architecture-designed structure aims to be more than just another musty old museum with manic school groups and curious retirees dutifully labouring past each dust-covered exhibit.

While the exterior resembles a Prairie snowdrift, the centre's interior elements were created by Montréal's Design + Communication Inc. to engage the paying public with interactive exhibits and impressive multimedia presentations.

Like that other dazzling Quebec export that put the fun back into circuses, D+C have reconfigured the museum experience. Forty years and more than 300 projects around the world later, they're known for an innovative approach to turn a potentially dull day at the museum into one driven by meaningful and resonant educational experiences.

If you've been to the centre of Canada's dinosaur universe, the Royal Tyrrell museum in Drumheller, Alta., then you'll recognize D+C's deft touch.

The multimedia show is presented in the custom-designed Carousel Theatre, a 125-seat facility with a 27-minute multimedia presentation. Headphones attached to the red serge theatre seats provide dialogue in both official languages. This bilingual sit-down show details the history of the RCMP, narrated by a holographic female RCMP constable who "just graduated from the Academy" and hovers at an adjacent podium.

After the theatre experience, visitors spill out into the ten main exhibits. The permanent collection, comprised of 33,000 artefacts from the Academy's Centennial Museum and long-term storage, displays the NWMP/RCMP from their beginnings in 1873 to the present.

The artefacts depict the RCMP's history, but it's also the story of The West, First Nations and Northern Canada. The most prominent exhibit is the "The March of the Mounties," a life-size sculpture composed of men, women, vehicles and iconic objects from the force's history that stretches the full 30-metre length of the main exhibition hall and anchors the key exhibit areas.

An interactive exhibit, "Cracking the Case," entertains and challenges anybody with its CSI-esque approach to solving crimes and upholds that reputation of how the Mountie "always gets his man."

Given some time, the Mounties' flashy tourist attraction might help to make them even more internationally recognizable than a bottle of Coke.

Details: *Visitors should set aside four hours to enjoy the "Mountie Museum." 5907 Dewdney Avenue. Open seven days 9 am – 5 pm. 1-866-567-7267 or (306) 522-7333, rcmpheritagecentre.com*

Surf, Turf & Nightcap   11

Within a few blocks of downtown Regina, from Scarth to Broad Streets, you can chopstick some authentic sushi, scarf a savoury steak and down a nightcap at the hottest downtown winebar.

Visitors who crave a sushi dinner can find the best fresh ocean fish east of Vancouver at **Michi Japanese Restaurant and Sushi Bar** (1943 Scarth St., 306-565-0141, michi.ca). Owner Toshi Shinmura, who imports Japanese chefs to create this little sushi house on the Prairie, provides an authentic traditional atmosphere to relax over warm sake and an eclectic dinner for two served on tasteful Japanese ceramics. Michi's green tea ice cream is a great closer to this seafood feast.

If red meat is more to your liking, the classic locale is **The Diplomat** (2032 Broad St., 306-359-3366, thediplomatsteakhouse.com). Owner John Makris has played host to politicians like Brian Mulroney and Rene Levesque, diplomats from around the globe have signed the guestbook and the lobby is rife with photos of celebrities like John Candy and Stage West dinner theatre alumni David Madden (the Partridge Family's agent, Reuben Kincaid).

The kitschy red booths are cozy and intimate, the wine cellar is the best-stocked in the province and Frank Sinatra croons away while you treat yourself to a classic Caesar cocktail and some mushroom caps, followed by a juicy filet mignon. For dessert, sample the strawberry flambé with ice cream and a coffee. Allow three hours for dinner since this is old school dining at its finest. Unfortunately, the new school bylaws means cigars must be enjoyed outside.

Now you're primed for a nightcap at the hottest downtown winebar. Right down the street from The Diplomat (and steps from the Hotel Saskatchewan's comfy beds) is **crave kitchen + wine bar** (1925 Victoria Ave., 306-525-8777). Crave has a fresh modern ambience, the best smart drinks in town and if you're strategically staying at the Hotel Sask, you can amble back without worrying about your blood alcohol content.

12	Staging Culture

Before home theatre systems, there was London's Globe Theatre where William Shakespeare presented hit play after hit play for enthusiastic audiences. You might have heard of this prolific bard.

There's also Regina's Globe Theatre, possibly named to keep the good box office mojo that Shakespeare has passed on to generations of theatre venues and playwrights ever since. If you're keen on live theatre, check out our Globe.

Founded in 1966 by Ken and

Sue Kramer, the Globe Theatre is Saskatchewan's first professional theatre company. Over 40 years later, this theatre mainstay is the province's largest performing arts organization that regularly pulls in an average of 60,000 patrons per season. It also serves as the regional theatre for Regina and southern Saskatchewan.

Housed in the Prince Edward Building in the city's downtown, this designated heritage site was built in 1906 and originally served as the Regina Post Office, as the RCMP headquarters and later as City Hall. In 1981, in its fourth and present incarnation, the Globe Theatre took over the second and third floors of the Prince Edward building.

The Globe Theatre offers two stages: a 406-seat theatre in the round main stage and for more than ten years, a 100-seat black box space where the theatre produces the Shumiatcher Sandbox Series, a showcase for new work, emerging artists and experimental theatre.

The six-play main stage program includes a minimum of three Canadian plays each season and an annual Christmas production which now runs for six to seven weeks and plays to more than 20,000 people in a city of only 200,000.

The Globe Theatre has developed and produced new work from Saskatchewan playwrights such as local Joey Tremblay and Poundmaker First Nation's Floyd Favel. It also stages classic plays like Shakespeare's *A Midsummer Night's Dream,* Tennessee William's *The Glass Menagerie* and accessible musicals like *Anne of Green Gables.*

In 2006, the Globe launched a series of educational initiatives under the umbrella of the Globe Theatre School. The programs include classes and training for children and teens, an internship program with the University of Regina Faculty of Fine Arts, a provincial outreach workshop program, "Globe on the Road," and in 2008, an actor conservatory training program.

Details: *The Globe Theatre is located at 1801 Scarth Street in downtown Regina. The Main Box Office is on the 4th floor and the theatre's Evraz Main Stage and Templeton Studio Cabaret are on the 2nd floor. Box Office: (306) 525-6400 or (866) 954-5623, globetheatrelive.com*

Friends of the Firkin — 13

Who says there isn't any decent beer produced in Saskatchewan? Perhaps you've never stumbled into — or stumbled out of — Regina's Bushwakker Brewpub.

Canadian beer writer Stephen Beaumont hails Bushwakker as one of Canada's top brewpubs and *The Globe and Mail* considers the Bushwakker to be one of Canada's top five brewpubs. Maybe it's time

you found out for yourself.

The Bushwakker Brewpub was created on the main floor of the Strathdee Building, a classic brick, stone and wood structure in what is now known as Regina's Old Warehouse District.

Named after Scottish immigrant businessman, James Strathdee, the Strathdee was built out of the rubble of the 1912 Great Regina Cyclone on the site of a former Chinese laundry.

Opened in 1914, the Strathdee Building is an impressive representation of the classical revival tradition of Regina's first generation of warehouses. The main floor contained offices and a display area for the Campbell, Wilson, Strathdee grocery business with a pressed tin ceiling. This impressive architectural element was restored to its original glory during the Bushwakker Brewing Company renaissance.

On January 25, 1991, the Bushwakker Brewing Company was officially opened, named after a group of cross-country skiing enthusiasts that set out on a 10-kilometre ski trek every winter Friday from the University of Regina. They called themselves "the Bushwhackers," which means "those who create their own trails."

Company president Bev Robertson, a skiing Bushwhacker and a member of a group of brewing enthusiasts that called themselves "the Bushwhacker Brewers," changed the brewpub spelling to "Bushwakker" to avoid any trademark problems and so they could blaze their own beer trail.

In Regina's only full-mash brewpub, Bushwakker patrons can expect to find beer brewed on the premises plus a menu of pub fare and Saskatchewan specialties. And, if you hit the right evening, you can expect to be entertained by live music such as Monday Night

Jazz or Wednesday Night Folk where patrons can sip and savour local and touring solo artists, duos and bands that play everything roots from blues to Americana country to Celtic.

Bushwakker's other special events offer patrons, both beer connoisseurs and neophytes, the opportunity to become familiar with food and beverage products such as single malt whiskies, classic beer styles, beer-related cuisine and ethnic cuisine.

On the First Firkin Friday (the first Friday happy hour each month), patrons become part of a ceremony where, lead by a piper, a small keg (firkin) of fresh ale is paraded through the pub. A volunteer drives a tap into the firkin with a handmade wooden maul, then patrons within a six-metre radius are soaked with escaping beer.

Bev Robertson, a former New Brunswicker, even puts on Doc Robertson's Lobster Night where he leads a June evening of seafood fare in the middle of the Prairies. Fresh, live lobsters are flown in for a date with a huge pot of salted, boiling water and served alongside fresh Bushwakker beer, of course.

Details: *Bushwakkers is located at 2206 Dewdney Avenue and is open Mon. to Thurs., 11 am–1 am and Fri.–Sat., 11 am to 2 am. Closed Sundays. (306) 359-7276, bushwakker.com*

14 Cathedral Village Arts Festival

After a long Prairie winter that sees most Reginans cooped up, a street festival in late spring is sure to bring 'em out. That's the case when Regina's 13th Avenue fills with local residents who mix it up with their fellow manic neighbours.

Bohemian types established the Cathedral Village Arts Festival in 1991, a six-day celebration of the arts, life and the spirit of community that attracts over 35,000 attendees each May in an avenue-clogging street fair.

Saskatchewan's premiere arts festival features performing, visual and literary arts plus crafts and other entertainment. This established event offers professional artists an opportunity to present their work to new audiences while emerging artists also share the spotlight and show off their talents. The Arts Fest allows kids and adults to create, participate and enjoy the diversity of the arts.

The Arts Fest concludes with a Saturday Street Fair along 13th Avenue with over 250 artisans, performance stages, participatory events such as "Funville," evening cabarets and performers in Holy Rosary Park.

The Cathedral Village Arts Festival, which operates as a committee of the Cathedral Area Community Association, is possible because of almost 300 volunteers from Regina's artistic, professional and business sectors. These dedicated individuals provide their ideas and expertise to create this eclectic community event every year.

Most importantly as an inclusive festival, due to generous support from the community, cultural organizations, businesses, corporations and the public, this allows free access to all events.

Details: *The Cathedral Village Arts Festival runs for six days in May around the Victoria Day weekend. For additional information: (306) 569-8744, cathedralartsfestival.ca*

Scientific Fun House 15

"It's educational!"

Don't you just hate it when someone corrals you into attending a museum with that tempting lure? But at the Saskatchewan Science Centre, they've piqued our scientific curiosity with some hands-on fun.

You can be a student of Saskatchewan geography while you mount their massive indoor climbing wall, feel what it's like to be a puck at ice level at a hockey game, take a virtual road trip to Mars, or learn about local fauna by gazing at the Wascana marshland, which this facility of fun overlooks in Wascana Centre.

If you want to study water management or green energy solutions, their permanent exhibits allow you to learn more about climate change and wind power in a concrete context.

An IMAX Theatre provides high definition screenings and the centre also plays host to travelling exhibits such as the stargazer favourite, "Eyes to the Skies," which celebrated the Year of Astronomy and screened at the Sasktel Max Theatre.

Also, when the blood sugar dips, the whole family can enjoy a casual gourmet meal at the innovative Zest Restaurant, located conveniently right in the Science Centre.

If you still want to learn more, the Science Centre offers day camps for curious kids on school holidays, and professional development days, September to June, and popular week-long day camps during July and August.

Details: *The Saskatchewan Science Centre is located at 2903 Powerhouse Drive, off Wascana Drive on the north side of Wascana Lake. Open seven days and on statutory holidays. (306) 522-4629, sasksciencecentre.com*

16   Subterranean Cinema

If it's a great art film, it doesn't matter where you watch it — even if it's playing in a 109-seat movie theatre in a basement.

Located in the Regina Public Library's downtown main branch, the RPL Film Theatre luckily exists because all of the city's independent movie theatres have unfortunately been closed, torn down, or converted to other uses.

The RPL Film Theatre's mandate is to screen the best of world cinema, which it certainly does with up to 15 films a month. Since it's Regina's only art house cinema, it endeavours to program something for everyone, from critically acclaimed contemporary and alternative cinema to Canadian, foreign and independent films and documentaries.

This is where you'll find the discerning movie-goer when the *Cannes Advertising Awards*, the latest European film from Lars von Trier, or a CanCon flick about suburban sprawl like Gary Burns' *Radiant City*, comes to town. You'll bump elbows with downtown hipsters, U of R students, librarians and married couples out on a much needed film date.

During the mid-1960s, the need for a permanent venue for film enthusiasts grew into a RPL program, which was a co-operative effort between the local Film Council and the National Film Board of Canada.

In 1975, the RPL Film Theatre was officially launched in its current location. Recent renovations continue the cinema's unadorned, NFB-screening-room decor. But once the lights are out for a film you've waited months to see, who really cares what the theatre looks like inside?

Regular patrons benefit when they purchase a Cinephile film pass and gift certificates are also available. Remember to stop by the ATM first since the RPL Film Theatre only accepts cash.

While you're waiting for the box office to open, check out the Dunlop Gallery on the main floor. This multi-purpose art gallery, built as part of the library's current location in 1964, exhibits both Canadian and international artists.

Details: T*he RPL Film Theatre is located downstairs in the Regina Central Library's main branch at 2311 12th Avenue across from Victoria Park. The box office opens 45 minutes before showtime. Prices include tax: children (under 14) $3; adults, $6 or $9 for a double feature; students (w/ valid student card) and seniors $5 or $7.50 for a double feature. (306) 777-6104, reginalibrary.ca/filmtheatre; Dunlop Art Gallery (306) 777-6040, dunlopartgallery.org*

Saskatoon

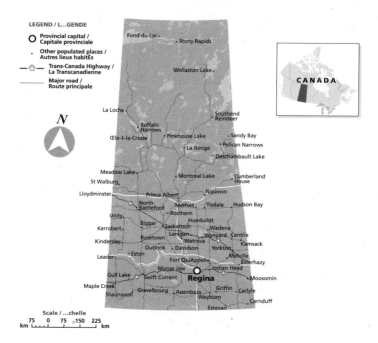

LEGEND / LÉGENDE

○ Provincial capital / Capitale provinciale

• Other populated places / Autres lieux habités

Trans-Canada Highway / La Transcanadienne

Major road / Route principale

N

CANADA

Scale / Échelle

75 0 75 150 225
km   km

Downtime in the Broadway District 17

In Saskatoon's original settlement, if you liked hedonistic weekends filled with drinking and debauchery, you wouldn't find it in the Paris of the Prairies. John Lake's teetotalling Temperance Colonisation Society arrived in 1882 from Toronto committed to establish a new city, Nutana, free of "alcohol's evil grip." You can just imagine what kind of buzz kill these folks were.

Nutana was eventually incorporated into the city of Saskatoon in 1906. Now not just for teetotallers these days, Saskatoon's vibrant Broadway District bops along to a contemporary beat. This hipster hub is where a day tripper can choose to relax in the city's best day spas, shop for clothing, shoes or locally produced home decor items, eat at gourmet restaurants or have a drink, if one pleases — all within four blocks.

Here are some of the Broadway District's best spots:

FASHION

Sandbox's first store at Waskesiu townsite in Prince Albert National Park is well known to Saskatonians. Sisters Colleen and Juanita's Saskatoon store, **Sandbox in the City**, is located in a former European car dealership where all generations of women can shop for an extensive selection of stylish clothing, shoes, purses and jewellery from Tribal, Kenneth Cole, Joseph Ribkoff and many others.

1002B Broadway Avenue, (306) 955-6600

BEAUTY

Ahava translates as "love" in Hebrew and the Broadway District's best day spa features a soothing profusion of services and aesthetics such as hydrotherapy and hot stones. If you have the time to really pamper yourself, spend four hours in their "Chocolate Spa Binge Package" or seven more in the "Ultimate Spa Package."

720 Broadway Avenue, (306) 978-8111, spaahava.com

GIFTS

Clay Studio Three was once three co-operative potters throwing Saskatchewan clay. Now there are over a dozen members and you're sure to find one to talk pottery with and help you find that one-of-a-kind, locally produced earthware gift, either functional or decorative. Priced from $15-$300, pit-fired and raku pottery are just two specialties.

#3-527 Main Street, (306) 242-1158, claystudiothree.com

HOME

A co-operative owned and operated by 11 Saskatoon artisans since 1974, **Handmade House** showcases unique handcrafted items — all in a very small space. Metal bowls, candleholders, raku pottery, wooden bread-boards, salad tongs, pillows, rag-rugs and many more Paris of the Prairies-produced items for your home. Even the walls are covered with tapestries, quilts and stained glass panels.

710 Broadway Avenue, (306) 665-5542, handmadehousesk.com

FOOD & DRINK

Tucked in beside the Broadway Theatre art cinema, **Calories Bakery and Restaurant** is the lunch and dessert spot during your Broadway District day trip. Executive chef Rémi Cousyn grew up in Provence and his classical French-inspired menu changes monthly to take advantage of fresh herbs and edible flowers from his own city garden and Saskatchewan organic producers. Owned and managed by Cousyn and his Saskatoon-born wife, Janis, this nationally recognized bistro and bakery also stocks many palate-pleasing wines.

721 Broadway Avenue, (306) 665-7991, caloriesrestaurants.com

Weczeria translates as "evening meal" in Polish, so for dinner, this small restaurant squirrelled in off Broadway Avenue serves an authentic Saskatchewan dining experience with a modern French flavour. Fresh and local ingredients and a constantly changing menu posted by chef-owner Daniel Walker spells new surprises every time you dine. Closed Sundays. *616 10th Street East, (306) 933-9600, weczeriarestaurant.ca*

The Yard & Flagon Pub is a funky, wood-panelled icon where professionals, university professors and their hip students rub elbows. This popular spot is perfect for an afternoon drink, a night-cap with friends or for the best chicken curry soup in Toon Town. The Y&F's rooftop deck is open April to October and blankets are provided on cooler evenings for those who haven't yet imbibed enough of the pub's extensive beer and liquor brands. *718 Broadway Avenue, (306) 653-8883*

Details: *The Broadway District's other numerous shops, services and watering holes are listed at onbroadway.ca*

18	The Meatpacker's Gift

What would Saskatoon be without the Mendel Art Gallery? It would be a city devoid of a major public art gallery to view the human condition expressed in so many forms.

The Mendel showcases contemporary and historical art, with exhibitions that rotate quarterly, while the permanent collection includes over 5,000 local, regional and national works of art.

So who was this Mendel? After Frederick (Fred) Salomon Mendel and his family fled Europe and Nazi oppression, they began a new life in Saskatoon when he founded Intercontinental Packers in 1940. Mendel had two divergent personas: meatpacking magnate and avid art collector. You could say Mendel was able to pack in some much needed culture into the Bridge City.

To make a public art gallery a reality, Fred Mendel made a generous financial donation to the city of Saskatoon. The government of Saskatchewan matched Mendel's monetary vision, a location was selected and a national design competition attracted 48 entries from architects across the country. The Winnipeg firm of Blankstein, Coop, Gillmor and Hanna won the contract and culture-starved Saskatonians and Saskatchewanians waited with baited breath.

Opened on October 16, 1964, the Mendel Art Gallery squats beside the South Saskatchewan River near the University Bridge, a Modernist landmark that includes a botanical conservatory, a welcome tropical refuge during a Prairie winter.

Mendel donated 13 Group of Seven paintings from his private collection to establish the gallery's permanent collection. Today it boasts more than 5,000 works, the largest public art collection in the province. Even hometown daughter and Renaissance woman, Joni Mitchell, has exhibited her paintings in the Mendel.

Luckily for the 150,000+ visitors in 2007, one of the highest per-capita attendance rates in Canada, the Mendel's mandate is "to operate and maintain a public museum for the collection, exhibition, preservation and interpretation of works of art and for the development of public understanding and appreciation of art."

TAKE5 PATRICIA HANBIDGE
A GARDENER'S FIVE EARTHLY DELIGHTS

Patricia Hanbidge, who has spent over 25 years in the horticultural industry as a consultant and teacher, once co-ordinated the Master Gardener Program, the Prairie Horticulture Certificate Program and the GardenLine Information Service at the University of Saskatchewan. She's the author of seven gardening books, writes a weekly syndicated newspaper column and her company, Green Schemes & Scapes, provides horticultural consulting and landscape design; she also imports and sells biological controls instead of toxic pesticides to help educate the public to use more sustainable gardening alternatives. To add an already full day, she also operates the Saskatoon School of Horticulture (growyourfuture.ca). Although we have a short growing season, Patricia says we still have many engaging public gardens worth visiting.

1. Honeywood (Dr. A.J. Porter) Heritage Nursery in Parkside. Founded in 1934, it's a small piece of Prairie history that should not be missed. Honeywood Nursery played an important role in developing horticulture in Western Canada. Dr. Porter was responsible for developing some of the first fruit varieties and ornamentals able to thrive on the Prairies yet he's best known for his hybridization of lilies. Open May through September, Honeywood Nursery is a Provincial Heritage Site that still displays the original log cabin and a beautiful array of lilies and other plants.

2. Prairie Farm Rehabilitation Administration (PFRA) Shelterbelt Centre in Indian Head. Yet another piece of Prairie history, the PFRA, operated by Agriculture and Agri-Food Canada, is devoted to promoting the benefits of integrating trees with agricultural systems plus it provides millions of seedlings to eligible clients. They

Saskatchewan River. In earlier days, this tranquil space was used for garden parties and croquet games.

Now this expansive green space is the site of numerous summer festivals including a major venue for the Sasktel Jazz Festival, community events and other special occasions.

Details: *601 Spadina Crescent East, (306) 244-5521 or 1-888-890-3222, deltahotels.com*

20 The Roxy Theatre's Classic Atmosphere

The interiors of today's big box movie theatres all look the same, but in the 1920s and 1930s, cinemas' architectural ambience meant movie-goers spent almost as much time staring at the ornate walls and ceiling as they did at the screen.

When the Roxy Theatre originally opened in 1930 in the heart of Saskatoon's Riversdale neighbourhood, it was one of hundreds of "atmospheric" movie theatres in Canada that included the iconic Capitol Theatre on 2nd Avenue South, which was demolished in 1978 so the unremarkable Scotia Centre could be built in its place. Now the Roxy Theatre is one of only a few atmospheric cinemas left.

The atmospheric cinema was an architectural design concept that emulated a fantastic foreign setting with an auditorium ceiling intended to give the illusion of an open sky as its defining feature.

In 2005, this cinematic treasure on 20th Street West was restored to its former glory through period touches such as a replica of the original Roxy Theatre sign and marquee. Artist Fred Harrison restored the ambience of a Spanish courtyard in the main auditorium through the use of colourful mural artwork.

Now part of the Rainbow Cinemas chain, the prices might have gone up since 1930, but $8 still buys you a ticket at this first-run cinema ($6 for a weekend matinee) that often runs independent art films.

The funky old theatre also hosts live and musical events, the party room is available for birthday parties and Rainbow Bear frequently crashes the Roxy's parties and matinees. Now that's atmosphere.

Details: *The Roxy Theatre is located at 320–20th Street West and offers free parking for evening shows just off 20th Street at Avenue D in a private lot. (306) 955-8642, rainbowcinemas.ca*

TAKE 5 ANDREA MENARD
FIVE CITY SANCTUARIES

Actor, singer, and writer Andrea Menard (andreamenard.com) stars in the supernatural crime drama, *Rabbit Fall*, which airs on SPACE and APTN. The film adaptation of her one-woman show, *The Velvet Devil*, debuted nationally on CBC Television's *Opening Night*. Andrea received a Gemini nomination for Best Performance by an Actress and also won Best Female Lead at the 2008 Showcase Awards where *The Velvet Devil* garnered 13 awards. Andrea has received a Gemini for Best Ensemble in an Animated Series for *Wapos Bay* plus a Gemini nomination for her leading role on *Moccasin Flats*. Andrea is also a recording artist who has released three albums, *The Velvet Devil*, *Simple Steps* and *Sparkle* with numerous nominations and awards that include the Western Canadian Music Awards and Canadian Aboriginal Music Awards. Andrea resides in Saskatoon with her best buds, Shady, a cockapoo and Gabe, a Bichon-Schitzou cross.

1. **Get your coffee (in a travel mug, not a take-out cup) and walk along Saskatoon's Meewasin Trail on the banks of the South Saskatchewan River**. Start at the Victoria Park boathouse, walk past the Riverworks Weir, and then all the way to G.D. Archibald Park. It's just long enough to recite your lines for an entire one-woman show! Oh, and your feet don't always have to be on concrete so pop down closer to the water and find some of the hidden trails. Actually, take your shoes off, and dip your feet in the river! As an actor, my career tends to change dramatically from year-to-year, so it's good to remember the piece of wisdom that "you never step into the same river twice," so just go with the flow!

2. **Go for a run around Regina's beautiful Wascana Lake**. When you feel the need to connect with nature, yet want to complete something tangible, a run around the entire lake takes less than 45 minutes. This is great when you're shooting a movie at the Canada-Saskatchewan Production Studios and need to recharge on your lunch break. Don't worry: someone will re-do your make-up when you return! Start and end at the Saskatchewan Legislative Building where you can breathe, limber up and then cool down on the wide stretch of lawn in front. Can't beat it!

3. **For a winter retreat, when you're up to your earmuffs in frigid weather, go to the Saskatoon Civic Conservatory, nestled in Saskatoon's Mendel Art Gallery.** It's like a tropical oasis complete with the sound of running water, the brilliant greens of tropical plants and the smell of wet earth. Very soothing and rejuvenating. I like to bring a script and a small pillow . . . you might stay longer than you think.

4. **Visit the Cathy Lauritsen Memorial Off-Leash Dog Park in Regina along Wascana Creek, south of 13th Avenue, beside the pathway.** The park is completely enclosed by a tall fence where a lovely trail runs in a circle around a big field. This is an ideal park to learn your lines because your dog can keep you on the trail while your head is planted in a script. No unexpected signposts, no busy streets, no cars, no cyclists . . . safe reading. And your dog will love you.

5. **The Devic Center for Environmental Harmony.** If you're scattered, and need a day to focus your artsy-fartsy brain, or you're broke and need to manifest more money, take a short drive west of Saskatoon for a sacred day at the Devic Center. This is a place where you can walk a rock-lain labyrinth out on the Prairie . . . for free. The smell of sage, the songs of the birds and the liberating walk itself reminds us that we are abundant and worthy of great things. Then go inside to Able Crystals & Therapies (ablecrystals.com) to view countless treasures, gemstones and books. Make sure you have a talk with owner Michael Stodola. He's definitely one of the treasures himself and he just might help you get your head on straight.

The Diefenbaker Canada Centre

My family connection with John Diefenbaker goes like this: when he was a young schoolboy in the Borden district near Saskatoon, he sat behind my paternal grandmother.

Once when Elsie May (Mayme) Henderson leapt up, waving her hand like a keener to answer a teacher's question, young John had cleverly secured her long pigtails to his wooden desk in anticipation of her popping up like a gopher. This mischievous youth also delighted in dunking those same pigtails in his desk-mounted inkwell.

In the 1970s at a political rally in Saskatoon, Diefenbaker, known for his astounding memory, still recognized my grandmother from his youth and called her by name.

Dief the Chief might be gone, but his legacy in Saskatchewan and his contribution to Canada lives on in Saskatoon at the Diefenbaker Canada Centre.

John G. Diefenbaker, Canada's 13th prime minister, secured a Conservative majority on March 31, 1958, the largest Parliamentary majority in Canadian history. Unfortunately, his charismatic political momentum was short-lived because like another recent Western Tory leader who was also born in Ontario — Stephen Harper — Diefenbaker was re-elected with only a minority government that eventually fell in 1963.

John Gordon Diefenbaker attended the University of Saskatchewan to become a lawyer. When he became Chancellor of the university in 1969, he announced his intention to bequeath his papers, memorabilia, personal library and the collection of another famous prime minister to his alma mater. Unlike some politicians, he stayed true to his word.

This museum, archives and research centre at the University of Saskatchewan, the only Prime Ministerial centre in the country, houses Diefenbaker's gravesite, memorabilia and personal collection.

The Diefenbaker Centre holds the personal papers, books and memorabilia collected by Diefenbaker during his lifetime (1895–1979). Dief was interested in all aspects of Canadian history and politics, particularly in Western Canada. He retained much of the correspondence and reference material that passed through his hands during an active political life that spanned 50 years.

The archives, which contain over three million documents, eight thousand photographs and two major press clippings collections, provide a unique record of Diefenbaker's life and Canadian history. Some of the personal collection of that other dynamic populist Tory, Sir John A. Macdonald, such as his original manuscripts, books, memorabilia and historic furniture, are also on display.

You can even eavesdrop on a recorded phone conversation from the early 1960s between Diefenbaker and U.S. President John F. Kennedy. Apparently the two never quite hit it off.

Beside these core collections, the centre also presents national and international cultural exhibitions, develops educational and public programs, which embrace the themes of Canadian citizenship, leadership and Canada's role in the international community.

If you're a political junkie or you just have a healthy curiosity about one of Saskatchewan's greatest exports, it's worth a visit. You can also visit Diefenbaker's first law office (1919–1925) in nearby Wakaw and his last home in Prince Albert; both are now museums.

Details: *Admission to the Diefenbaker Canada Centre includes a 30-minute guided tour: Adult $7; Senior/Student/Child $5; Family $15, (306) 966-8384, artsandscience.usask.ca/diefenbaker*

22 Lighting the Way

No, the Synchrotron isn't the Police's last album before Sting went solo. The Synchrotron, actually known as the Canadian Light Source (CLS), is a stadium-sized structure constructed on the grounds of the University of Saskatchewan as Canada's national facility for synchrotron light research.

Built for $173 million and opened in 2004, the synchrotron is one of the largest science projects in Canadian history. It's a collaboration of the federal, provincial and municipal governments plus universities from across the country and the private sector.

Some say the Canadian Light Source will "light the way" to a new era of science and innovation, which is true since its primary goal is to contribute to the quality of life around the world. The Canadian Light Source employs over 130 people: scientists, engineers, technicians and administrative personnel. For research collaborations, the CLS's location between the University of Saskatchewan's main campus and Innovation Place — one of Canada's leading high-tech industrial parks — is advantageous.

The CLS offers public and group tours of a facility that resembles a better-lit version of Jonathan Pryce's duct-riddled apartment block in *Brazil*, Terry Gilliam's dystopian 1985 film.

So what is a synchrotron anyway and what does this enigmatic facility do? And how come it cost $173 million to build? The synchrotron is a huge, doughnut-shaped ring that accelerates a stream of electrons and manipulates them to create a beam of light billions of times brighter than the sun. The rare light is harnessed by industrial and university researchers as a revolutionary new tool to observe structures and chemical reactions at a molecular level.

Synchrotrons can be used to analyse a host of physical, chemical, geological and biological processes. Researchers use this information to develop ways to reduce greenhouse gases, clean up mining wastes, examine the structure of surfaces to develop more effective paints and motor oils, design new drugs, develop new materials for products that range from solar panels to safer medical implants and build more powerful computer chips.

Since Gene Roddenberry correctly said that space is the final frontier, synchrotron experiments can even help with the search for other life in the universe.

Details: *Unlike most science centres, you can't just take a synchrotron tour every hour on the hour. Tours must be requested by contacting outreach@lightsource.ca. Learn more about the Canadian Light Source at lightsource.ca*

Meewasin Valley Trail   23

According to a 2004 study by the UK's Nature and Psychological Well-being, "within urban and semi-urban settings, access to green, open spaces can have a beneficial effect."

Fortunately, Saskatoon's early city planners already figured that out when they decided the river valley should be largely left to the enjoyment of its citizens. So did the provincial government when they created the Meewasin Valley Authority (MVA), a conservation organization dedicated to conserving the natural and cultural heritage resources of the South Saskatchewan River Valley in and around Saskatoon.

While Meewasin's jurisdiction does centre in Saskatoon, it actually runs approximately 60 kilometres along the river through Saskatoon, the R.M. of Corman Park and from Pike Lake in the southwest to Clarke's Crossing in the northeast. It encompasses over 40 square kilometres which includes the South Saskatchewan River, conservation areas, parks, museums, interpretive centres, the University of Saskatchewan lands, canoe launches, community links plus the Meewasin Valley Trail.

Meewasin, Plains Cree for "beautiful," stretches for 21 kilometres along the South Saskatchewan River through central Saskatoon where you'll find plenty of parks for intimate picnics and family barbeques. This undulating riparian ribbon also serves as a peaceful path for day hikes, an ideal path for runners and cyclists plus it's an accessible track for cross-country skiers.

The Meewasin Skating Rink, located beside the historic Bessborough Hotel, operates 100 days per season and skates are complimentary, though donations are gladly accepted.

Check out the Meewasin Valley Authority's website for trail maps and get moving Meewasin-style.

Details: *The Meewasin Valley Interpretive Centre is a great start-off point. 402 Third Avenue South, (306) 665-6888, meewasin.com*

24 | Market Frenzy

In opposition to a world of big box generica and strip malls, more urban Saskatchewanians are grabbing their reusable fabric grocery bags and heading for their local farmers' market.

What's led them there? Taste, quality, freshness, price and increased consumer interest in supporting local, often organic, farms and producers whose food has travelled fewer kilometres.

The weekend farmers' market is a good example of Saskatchewanians' continuing connection with the land, the satisfying search for quality ingredients and the chance to mingle with other like-minded people.

The Saskatoon Farmers' Market is a member-owned, non-profit co-operative that provides Saskatonians and visitors the best in local agricultural products, baking, prepared foods and crafts. The Market was founded in 1975 on the basic principle that members must make, bake or grow whatever they're selling. This provides the customer with an opportunity to deal directly with the producer.

In 2007, the Saskatoon Farmers' Market moved to its year-round location at River Landing inside a renovated former electrical garage once operated by the City of Saskatoon.

Shoppers at this established farmers' market can find elk, venison,

bison paté and saskatoon berry products, with selection and prices often lower than standard retail outlets.

Adjacent to the facility, the "Market Square" allows for summer outdoor markets and special events. Once you've filled your grocery bags with the local bounty, you can hang around for special events that include live music, local chefs demonstrating their skills, prize give-aways and family entertainment.

During reduced hours in the winter, a new concept called the "Little Market Store" carries a selection of vendor products such as preserves, sauerkraut, pickled vegetables, jewellery, flaxseed, frozen soups, perogies, cabbage rolls, pottery, crafts, beef, fish plus eggs and baking when available.

Details: *The Saskatoon Farmers' Market is open on selected days year-round. (306) 384-6262, saskatoonfarmersmarket.com*

Shakespeare On A Golf Course 25

Every summer, Saskatchewanians gather at a temporary Medieval Village perched on the South Saskatchewan River in Saskatoon to celebrate and re-enact the words of The Bard.

For a few hours, local actors and audience members commune in a big white tent at the foot of the 25th Street Bridge. To pull off just one season of Shakespeare on the Saskatchewan, it takes three years of planning so this July to mid-August festival is a must-see. Past performances include *A Midsummer Night's Dream*, *Twelfth Night*, *Romeo and Juliet*, *King Lear* and *The Tempest*.

What makes this brief season of outdoor Shakespeare more accessible is the brave decision to occasionally veer from the traditional interpretation of Shakespeare's plays. In seasons past, the directors have elected to update the plays via heavy metal or punk rock music as a backdrop. In 1985, the first year the outdoor theatre company mounted a production, *A Midsummer's Night Dream* was set on a golf course.

On select nights, for those with a hearty appetite, you can savour a medieval feast prior to the show onsite at the "Elizabethan Village." It features live entertainment, gourmet cuisine and a mug of grog, of course, which is also available at Sir Toby's Tavern, which is open every night of the festival.

Details: *Shakespeare on the Saskatchewan, which runs for six weeks from early July to mid-August, is located at the foot of the 25th Street Bridge near the Mendel Art Gallery. (306) 652-9100, shakespeareonthesaskatchewan.com*

26 All That Jazz And More

It's not a Saskatchewan summer without a jazz festival. Luckily, we have one. In 1992, the Saskatchewan Jazz Festival (SJF) was created by the Saskatoon Jazz Society with a mandate to stage an "artistically significant annual festival of jazz and related music." They've certainly succeeded.

Every year for ten days in late June, the Saskatchewan Jazz Festival, a non-profit organization and registered charity, attracts more than 60,000 jazz enthusiasts to enjoy live jazz and blues from world-renowned artists. You can experience this music at several ticketed and free venues spread around Saskatoon plus a few in Regina and North Battleford.

From indoor shows at the Broadway Theatre by American alto saxophonist David Sanborn to outdoor performances by Johnny Winters and Sonny Rollins at the Bessborough Gardens, our little jazz fest on the Prairies keeps bringing in the best of the best. Established legends like five-time Grammy Award winner Buddy Guy share the Jazz Festival with relative neo-crossover, rap n' roller newcomers like Vancouver-based K-os.

The Saskatchewan Jazz Festival has also attracted other top names in the last few years like Canadian blueswoman Sue Foley, Robert Cray, Sonny Rhodes and the Neville Brothers.

While the draw is to bring in "name brand" musicians to sell tickets, the festival also provides opportunities for the professional development of Saskatchewan musicians plus a variety of educational experiences for the people of Saskatchewan. Check out our Jazz Fest for some amazing shows for a small ticket price in intimate settings and support a good cause at the same time.

Details: *The Saskatchewan Jazz Festival is staged annually for ten days from late June to early July. Buy tickets by phone or online. (306) 975-8398 or 1-877-975-8398, saskjazz.com*

Sure you can view a movie on your cellphone, but the Broadway Theatre lets you experience that Cannes award-winning film that everybody is talking about in New York and Toronto in a real cinema setting. You know, old school, seated beside other film enthusiasts and a big screen.

Built in 1946, the Broadway Theatre in the Nutana neighbourhood supplied post-war cinemaphiles with popular movies of the day. Live music performances were also staged in front of the movie screen. The Broadway Theatre operated with this successful format until the late 1970s when it ran into corporate cinema competition.

In response, the owners tried to mimic New York's Times Square of the time and run soft-core porn movies. I remember a high school friend who apprenticed as a projectionist and screened the favourites of the day like *Emmanuel* and *Deep Throat* at the then seedy Broadway — even though he wasn't old enough to actually buy a ticket.

Luckily, that format was short-lived. By 1984, the Broadway got another shot at its former glory when it was turned into a repertory movie house and live performance venue. Sadly, the Broadway's art house format lasted less than ten years. When it locked its doors for possibly the last time, the story received so much media coverage that even the editors at *The Globe and Mail* saw to run it in their front section.

That's when the non-profit Friends of the Broadway Theatre was formed. By October 1993, 4,500 film fans had purchased membership discount cards despite the fact the Broadway may have never re-opened. The Broadway, now community-owned and operated, has continued to operate with a strong 1,500–2,000 membership base.

Although primarily a repertory cinema, the Broadway also serves as the home of the Flicks International Children's Film Festival and the Saskatoon Soaps Improvisational Theatre Troupe. It's also a primary stage during the annual Broadway Comedy-Busking Festival and a major venue during the Saskatoon Fringe and Saskatchewan Jazz festivals.

Details: *The Broadway Theatre is located at 715 Broadway Avenue. Film and event info can be accessed through the Info Line or their website: (306) 384-3456, broadwaytheatre.ca*

28   Do the Hokey-Pokey

If you're greeted by a ballerina on stilts or pass a tree that actually houses the Green Man, you're at the Saskatchewan Children's Festival. This annual event is like a folk music festival for the under-aged set — minus the beer tent.

In yet another riverside festival (this one is in early June), a Saskatoon park becomes a wonderland for kiddies where 20,000 guests and performers gather at Kiwanis Park near the Bessborough Hotel.

Since 1988, this four-day multimedia festival of performing arts has featured first-rate main-stage entertainment, a science camp, fossil finds, the Mendel Art Caravan, origami, face painting, chalk art, a labyrinth and a story tent.

Recent performers have included folkie and Juno Award-winner Connie Kaldor, Bobs and Lolo (who sing about bikes and bugs, raindrops and recycling), the Acadian fiddle performers Grand Derangement, West African master musicians Masabo!, Brazilian

clown O Cano! (who juggles, plays with found objects and performs acrobatics) and local mainstay Prairie Dog Doug who performs his "Songs from the Silly Side of Saskatchewan" and leads the audience in the hokey-pokey dance.

Bring the kids and your inner child to enjoy this wacky and wonderful outdoor circus by the river.

Details: *The Saskatchewan Children's Festival is held in early June, rain or shine, at Kiwanis Park near the Bessborough Hotel on Spadina Crescent. (306) 664-3378, saskatchewanchildrensfestival.ca*

Riverside Theatre 29

The Persephone Theatre's founders either named themselves after the Greek Goddess of fertility and agriculture — a perfect moniker for a successful theatre company in a sodbuster province — or after Nick Adonidas' beat-up boat on CBC Television's long-running series, *The Beachcombers*.

Launched in 1974, the Persephone Theatre has expanded over the years and has now settled into their scenic new River Landing location near 2nd Avenue South. The state-of-the-art facility seats 450 with an additional black box theatre that accommodates 100.

This dynamic setting is the ideal venue for live theatre since guests can stroll the Meewasin Valley Trail before enjoying a performance. Once inside the facility, you can bask in the light from the massive windows or enjoy a river view with a pre-show glass of merlot.

Persephone's regular season includes six classic and contemporary works from both a national and international repertoire. The busy theatre's recent productions include *The Walnut Tree, Little Women, The Full Monty* and *Billy Bishop Goes to War*, yet strangely, still no sign of a stage production of *The Beachcombers*, even with a handy adjacent waterway.

Details: *The Persephone Theatre is located at 100 Spadina Crescent East (the south end of 2nd Ave. S, off 19th St.). (306) 384-2126, persephonetheatre.org*

30 Star Struck at the U of S

There's no better way to bring yourself down to size in the universe than to peer through an observatory telescope. Luckily, we've had one in place for over 80 years — and peeks are free.

During the week, telescopes and other scientific equipment at the Campus Observatory are used by University of Saskatchewan students for the laboratory component of their courses. But on Saturday evenings, the Observatory facilities are available to campus visitors to view our night sky.

The Campus Observatory was constructed in two phases between 1928 and 1930 for $23,000. Much of the funding was supplemented by private donations, many from recognizable Saskatoon residents, and a plaque with the donors' names still hangs inside the Observatory's dome.

The Observatory houses a three-metre long refracting telescope with a 15-centimetre diameter lens. Yes, size does matter. On clear Saturday evenings, staff will point the telescope at seasonal objects in the sky. That's when the eye-popping sights begin: planets, nebulae, star clusters, galaxies and if you're lucky, even comets can be viewed at the right time of year.

However, not every night will be wide open to the stars. If it's a cloudy evening, staff put on an educational slide show that depicts objects in our solar system, galaxy and beyond.

The Observatory also encompasses a small museum that serves as a tour of our solar system and features exhibits that highlight the history and fundamentals of astronomy, including a black hole display.

The Campus Observatory will encourage you to adopt a star — and they don't mean a Hollywood star. Stars are adopted through a tax-deductible contribution to the University of Saskatchewan. Adoption rates depend upon the star's brightness (again, not Hollywood stars) and prices range from $50 to $1,500. Your donation helps to purchase and maintain the University of Saskatchewan's telescopes, facilities and to hire personnel so these important astronomy programs can continue in the community.

Details: *The Campus Observatory is open to the public on Saturday evenings. Viewing times alternate according to the season (based on hours of light per day), so check first before visiting. Special tours may be arranged during the summer months. Located on the U of S campus, 1 block north of the intersection of Wiggins Avenue and College Drive. (306) 966-6396, physics.usask.ca/observatory*

Foodie Party in the Park | 31

If they cook it, you will come. This seems to be the approach of over 30 Saskatoon restaurants when they gather for six days every July to show off their creations in Kiwanis Park. And we're there to gobble them up.

Since 1995, A Taste of Saskatchewan, designed after three very successful, long-running foodie festivals in Edmonton, Winnipeg and that gastronomic pioneer, A Taste of Chicago, aims to follow the same concept of providing an urban, outdoor dining and entertainment event in the height of summer.

Here's how it works in Toon Town: each restaurant is limited to serving three items, which are the restaurant's house favourites. A Taste of Saskatchewan sells food tokens to the public for $2/each then these food tokens are exchanged at the restaurant's kiosk for their desired food items. They also sell beverage tokens, both alcoholic and non-alcoholic.

All food items are priced at one or two tokens with generous portions, so this foodie party in the park means A Taste of Saskatchewan is an affordable stop for hungry diners.

Everyone is invited to attend and if the smorgasbord of choices isn't enough, there's free live music and special prize packages supplied by the event's sponsors.

While the biggest crowds are on the weekend, Tuesday to Friday is perfect for those who work in the downtown area or who are visiting Saskatoon to drop in and enjoy lunch in this *al fresco* setting, serenaded by live entertainment.

Details: *Kiwanis Park, the annual setting for A Taste of Saskatchewan, is located along the South Saskatchewan River near the Bessborough Hotel. (306) 975-3175, tasteofsaskatchewan.ca*

32   The Fringe

Standing in line with friends, one hour before show time, you realize those rush $10-seating tickets and the mysterious international theatre company whose work you're about to experience sums up the grassroots Fringe experience. But you're still ready to come out every year to support it.

In the summer of 1989, the first-ever Saskatoon Fringe Theatre Festival was staged at the Duchess Street theatre venue by the 25th Street Theatre Company. In 1990, the Fringe moved to Broadway District venues where it's remained ever since.

Every year, for four days in the height of midsummer, over 40,000 people descend on the trendy Broadway District to dine out, wander Broadway Avenue and take in this popular alternative theatre festival in support of indie theatre. Rush tickets, which are available at theatre venues an hour before each show, serves to keep tickets easily accessible for Fringe attendees.

The Saskatoon Fringe annually hosts about 50 global theatre companies that encompass over 200 individual performers and company members. So they can continue to hone their craft and show up again next year, all participating theatre groups keep 100 percent of Fringe ticket proceeds.

The Saskatoon Fringe Theatre Festival is part of a larger international movement of Fringe festivals. This touring circuit, whose tradition began with Scotland's Edinburgh Fringe Festival in 1947, now includes worldwide festivals from Athens to Grande Prairie.

Get your hands on a festival guidebook or visit their website so you can map out your Fringe plans and see some great grassroots theatre firsthand — all for $10 or less per show.

Details: *The Fringe is staged in Saskatoon's Broadway District at a variety of venues in late July and early August. (306) 653-7701, 25streettheatre.org*

A Cut Above The Rest   33

Ensconced in the Sheraton Cavalier Hotel, Carver's Steakhouse isn't one of those hotel restaurants that serve food right out of a microwave in a dining room badly in need of a décor update.

Instead, this award-winning Saskatoon hot spot, centred around a three-sided fireplace, serves up exceptional meals with top quality ingredients accompanied by an extensive list of wines and always served in Riedel crystal.

You'll find local foodies and visiting business people on expense accounts enjoying meals often sourced from Saskatchewan's local bounty, those small regional suppliers who produce free-range chicken, Saskatchewan steelhead trout and other fresh flavours.

Carver's Steakhouse is known, not surprisingly, for its Sterling Silver Premier Beef. These 28-day aged "AAA" Steak & Prime Rib Cuts, hand-carved and specially selected for Carver's, originate from free-range, Canadian Prairies beef.

When seasonally available, you'll even see game meats like elk and wild boar from Saskatchewan breeders on the menu along with fresh local produce.

Details: *Carver's Steakhouse is located in the Saskatoon Sheraton Cavalier Hotel at 612 Spadina Crescent East. Reservations are strongly recommended. (306) 652-6770, sheraton.com/saskatoon*

34   Farm to Fork

At one time, fresh ingredients used to arrive in Saskatchewan's local markets and restaurants directly from area farms. After a prolonged period where imported and processed food reigned, the good old days are back again at Souleio Foods.

Souleio (soo-lee-o) Foods is a culinary partnership between Saskatoon's Calories Restaurant — a veteran bastion of fresh, inspired cuisine in the Broadway District — and the all-natural food expertise of Pine View Farms in the nearby Mennonite community of Osler.

Calories Restaurant originally began to sell the Souleio Foods brand in 2007, which is a product line of high-quality organic food products with a social and regional economics philosophy.

In June 2009, the husband and wife teams of chef Rémi and Janis Cousyn of Calories and Kevin and Melanie Boldt of Pine View Farms, launched their retail store in downtown Saskatoon.

Rémi Cousyn grew up in Provence, France and polished his chef skills over 17 years in France, Switzerland and Canada before moving to Saskatoon in 1995.

Souleio, which means "sun" in the Provençale dialect, represents life's bounty. The Cousyns and the Boldts' food mission is to create superior organic products that derive directly from the farm-gate and local crafter. Souleio emphasizes, in all aspects of its business, the important link between the sharing of food and quality of life while they provide the consumer with a local alternative.

The Souleio philosophy is that when you support your local farmers, crafters and independent businesses, you make a difference that trickles down to both rural and city centre revitalization.

Foodies can source all the organic staples from milk, bread, eggs and cheese, to meats, deli and even many foods crafted in their in-store bakery. Souleio also features a quick-serve restaurant with a dine-in area, catering, private dining, curbside valet pick-up and takeout service.

The mouth-watering products include Souleio's signature soup, spicy merguez all-natural lamb sausage, all-natural chicken pesto sausage, handmade chocolates, flax cookies plus fruit preserves and jellies.

The retail location is a labour of love for the two couples. After four years of planning and six months of renovations to the historic McLean Building — restoring a 1911 building for modern use — Souleio Foods is the ideal grocery and dining spot for discerning Saskatchewanians.

Details: *Souleio is located at 265 3rd Avenue South between 20th and 21st Streets. Open Mon. – Fri., 7 am – 7 pm, Sat. 8 am – 7 pm with private dining after 7 pm. Closed Sundays. (306) 979-8102, souleio.com, caloriesrestaurants.com, pineviewfarms.com*

Central

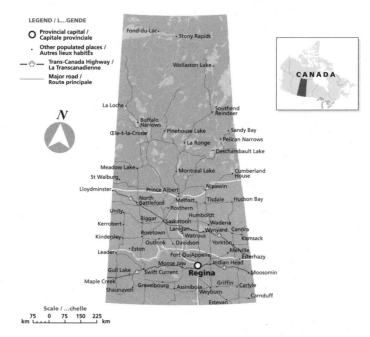

Moose Jaw's Oasis	35

For many Canadian tourists, southern Saskatchewan in the summer is a sunny, mostly flat region of big skies and endless Trans-Canada Highway drives.

But for the adventurous or simply road-weary traveller in search of a natural mineral spa, the Prairie heartland offers two distinct experiences: a simple soak in a buoyant lake at Manitou Beach or the amenities of an upscale spa hotel in Moose Jaw.

Moose Jaw's Temple Gardens Mineral Spa Resort Hotel is conveniently located down the hill from the Trans-Canada highway. Established in 1996, this 179-room resort downtown on Fairford

Street East includes a luxury hotel, a natural mineral pool high above the street and the Oasis Spa where pampering services range from body wraps, facials and a full range of massage treatments.

Chicago gangster Al Capone is rumoured to have "gone to the mattresses" in this Prairie city when things got too hot in the Windy City. Gambling and moving liquor were once the sole purview of Moose Jaw's Prohibition-era gangsters; now the government-owned Saskatchewan Liquor & Gaming Authority has taken over their old turf with Casino Moose Jaw, a 2002 addition connected to the hotel by a skywalk.

When Moose Jaw's pioneer families arrived in 1882, they didn't originally spot steam and a body of hot water. Moose Jaw's mineral springs were discovered in 1910 by oil drillers. Instead of hitting black crude, vast amounts of hot, mineral-rich water came up instead. The drillers had tapped into water-soaked porous rock, the remnants of an ancient seabed.

The city soon capitalized on the mineral springs by building an indoor "natatorium" in the downtown core and for many years it attracted savvy soakers from around the region for the "taking of waters."

In 1980, the city drilled a new geo-thermal well, which provides Temple Gardens with its therapeutic waters. The water travels through an insulated pipeline from the wellhead, about a kilometre from the resort. The minerals in the waters are similar to the popular hot springs in the Rockies (Banff, Radium and Miette) that contain magnesium sulphate, sodium, potassium and calcium.

The city's name translates from the Cree word "Moosegaw," meaning "warm breezes." Today's warm underground breezes can be found inside the Temple Garden's sizeable pool on the top of the hotel with those mineral-rich, geo-thermal waters. When it's time to change the water, Temple Gardens even have a recycling program where they actually treat the water before it's piped back underground so that it becomes a renewable resource.

Guests have full access to the mineral pool plus the outdoor pool facility, a smaller extension of the indoor pool — but with much hotter mineral-rich water. Open from 7 am to 11 pm, it's the place to either thaw out after surviving a lengthy Arctic front or a soak under the stars before turning in for the night. Like the Oasis Spa, it's open to the public.

Details: *Temple Gardens Mineral Spa Resort Hotel is open year-round in downtown Moose Jaw. 24 Fairford Street East, 1-800-718-7727, templegardens.sk.ca*

36 Subterranean Moose Jaw

Most year-round tourism destinations in Saskatchewan can't boast a winter visit without a snorkel parka and Sorel snowboots.

The Tunnels of Moose Jaw tours can. Their two (mostly under-

TAKE 5 LITTLE MISS HIGGINS
A MUSICIAN'S FIVE VENUES THAT STRIKE A CHORD

Singer/lead guitarist Little Miss Higgins (aka Jolene) and acoustic guitarist Foy Taylor (David Mark) take audiences back into late 1930s–1940s America with their old timey country blues and theatrical stage approach. Little Miss Higgins' muse is the late American country blues crooner, Memphis Minnie, yet the duos' song themes are inspired and rooted squarely in Western Canada. Bluesman Big Dave McLean says she's "a true jewel of the Canadian Prairies." Pick up their two studio CDs, *Cobbler Shop Sessions* and *Junction City*, their recent live effort, *Two Nights In March*, or catch this Nokomis-based songbird and her sideman on tour (littlemisshiggins.com).

1. **The Nokomis Hotel Bar (also known as the "Beverage Room")**. Built in the early 1900s, this small town hotel features a small stage but a big heart. Bands travelling through or from around the province have performed in the "woodsy" setting of this bar, including the resident, or regular, Little Miss Higgins and partner Foy Taylor. With only nine hotel rooms, sleeping over can be a challenge, but it's always a good time.

2. **Pumpjacks in Weyburn**. A cozy venue with great food and music where your drink is never empty.

3. **Danceland in Manitou Beach**. This amazing old dance hall still hosts performances and dances. Just the building itself is worth the venture. Then, to top it off with live music, it's a sight to see.

4. **Amigo's in Saskatoon**. Lots of music and fabulous food. A great place to spend an evening with friends and make new ones.

5. **E. A. Rawlinson Centre in Prince Albert**. This is a beautiful, newer theatre space with amazing acoustics and not a bad seat in the whole place.

ground) tunnel tours carry you to another time and place before legal casinos and spa gangs took over The Friendly City.

The most well known of the two is The Chicago Connection tour. Moose Jaw was notorious, especially in the 1920s, when Prohibition was at its peak and illegal booze and prostitution reigned. Iconic gangster Al Capone was rumoured to sneak off to Moose Jaw when things got too hot in Chicago; the Soo Line once ran directly from Chicago to Moose Jaw, which was a major rail hub in Western Canada.

The Chicago Connection story covers that infamous period and you get to play a character in this interactive tour. Big Al's people are in Moose Jaw from the States to buy some illegal booze from you. This is your chance to step into the role of the bootlegger and live the danger and excitement of the illegal entrepreneur under the streets of downtown Moose Jaw.

The tour features guides in character and period costume, authentic sets within a tunnel matrix, multimedia, animatronics and special effects. These elements combine to create an atmosphere of life in the booze business during Moose Jaw's rough and tumble Prohibition period of the 1920s.

The second tour, Passage to Fortune, takes you to an even earlier period when indentured Chinese immigrants worked and lived in dingy, underground laundries and they smoked opium in their downtime to help them escape from their daily drudgery.

These men from impoverished Chinese provinces borrowed money from unscrupulous people in China to emigrate to Canada; they spent years working it off underground in commercial laundries and at other menial jobs.

Set in late 19th century Moose Jaw, this tour profiles the hardships of Chinese immigration to the Canadian Prairies, which also witnessed other non-British emigration during that period. These immigrants from China, who stuck out amongst a sea of Europeans, came to a new land where hard laws and attitudes forced them underground.

In this tour's role playing, you become one of those indentured laundry workers who is treated harshly by a stern, middle-aged British-Canadian woman (a guide in character).

You're immersed in the sights, the sounds and the secrets of that time with dingy sets within the tunnels, multimedia, animatronics and special effects.

To maintain the historical period theme during your time in Moose Jaw, I suggest some historical accommodations.

Capone's Hideaway Motel

Although the motel concept didn't actually appear until the 1940s, the Capone's Hideaway Motel is still running with the 1920s Prohibition theme. Guests, who look for the bright yellow-and-black 1920s road car anchored to a ten-metre high pole in the parking lot, are treated to three theme rooms with early twentieth century furniture and other period touches like double beds. Couples who need more room can ask for the queens or one king available in the non-theme rooms. Capone's Hideaway Motel is located only one block from the Tunnels of Moose Jaw Tours.

1 Main Street North, (306) 692-6422

Wakamow Heights Bed & Breakfast

While in Moose Jaw, tunnel tourists can also stay at the historical Wakamow Heights B&B (circa 1908), built by one of Moose Jaw's prominent early families. Wellington and Olive White owned the Moose Jaw Brick Company and later, the White Pools at Little Manitou Lake, which competed with the Banff Springs for summer natural springs business in the 1920s. Check out the B&B's engaging history on their website.

690 Aldersgate Street East, (306) 693-9963, wakamowheights.com

Details: *Each Tunnel Tour is about 50 minutes. Rain, shine or blizzard, the show must go on — except Christmas Day. Dates and times are subject to change without notice; call first or check the website. 18 Main Street North, (306) 693-5261, tunnelsofmoosejaw.com*

Downtown Moose Spa 37

Once a rough-and-tumble city during its notorious Prohibition past, rife with criminal gangs and corrupt police, Moose Jaw is now better known for mineral springs and luscious gardens.

Downtown Moose Jaw or "Moose Spa" also boasts lovingly preserved Victorian architecture, the classic Crescent Park, fashion-forward shops and a relaxed vibe in this Prairie diamond in the rough. Blame it on The Friendly City's spa culture.

Here are some of the best spots downtown, from fashion to design to spas, of course.

Moose Couture

This mainstay of casual and elegant style in the historic Hammond building features Montréal designers Frank Lyman, Cartise and Nueva, bamboo fabrics from B.C.'s Lela Designs and import lines Renuar, Orly, Svetlana and Linea Domani. Owner Liz Craigen also keeps her shelves well-stocked with Kathy Van Zealand purses, Luv shoes, natural stone jewellery from local designer Krisztina Makko plus home decor items.

Cranberry Rose Boutique, 316 Main St. North, (306) 693-7779, cranberryrose.com

Naughty Yet Nice

If it were still Moose Jaw's scandalous Prohibition era, gangster molls would shop in cheeky proprietor Patricia McKibben's lingerie store, Pillow Talk. Her former drug store location on Main Street now dispenses lingerie, bras and hosiery for all sizes from Change, Escante, Love Lines, Bamboo Nights, Silks, Coconut Grove and Coquette. Non-frilly items include Kama Sutra oil, edible body soufflés, Wild Prairie soaps and even some naughty duds for the men folk.

Pillow Talk Lingerie, 20 Main St. N. (306) 692-8890, pillowtalklingerie.com

That's a Wrap

25+ day spas operate in Saskatchewan's fourth largest city. Moose Jaw's Victorian spa focuses on relaxation. Set in an historic home across from the swan-friendly Crescent Park, owner Athena Cutts offers soothing packages and salon services for locals and road-weary Trans-Canada motorists. After pre-treatment tea in the parlour, experience the Rosehip Oil or Hot Seamud Body Wraps — both include a 30-minute post-wrap massage. Don't even attempt to operate heavy equipment after your relaxing session.

New Element Relaxation Spa & Salon, 436 Langdon Crescent, (306) 692-1321, newelementspa.com

Next Stop: Bali

When it's −40 degrees in Saskatchewan, an authentic Balinese spa looks pretty appealing. Sahara's 2,500-square-metre space within a renovated railway station replicates the 200+ spas of Bali, Indonesia. Exotic oil blends and Jamu products are applied by certified Jamu therapists in Canada's only Jamu spa. For some spa downtime with your partner, try out the couples' room and the three-hour Ultimate Indulgence treatment.

Sahara Spa, 341 Stadacona St E., (306) 692-1012, saharaspa.ca

Heartland Chic

Located safely away from the nearby recliner and loveseat vendors, Jillian's selection of contemporary home decor is ambitious for such a small burg. This twenty-something interior decorator sells urban

TAKE 5 JOHN GORMLEY
FIVE GOLF COURSES WORTH THE DRIVE

John Gormley, a lawyer and former Member of Parliament, is also the host of Saskatchewan's top-rated commercial radio talk show, "John Gormley Live," heard weekday mornings on Saskatoon's News Talk 650 CKOM and Regina's News Talk 980 CJME. John covers everything from politics to pop culture to the day's top stories and controversies. His main passion in non-snowy times is golf and he's the first to admit that he's not very good at it. This list comes with two caveats: John has probably golfed 35 Saskatchewan courses, but in Canada's most golf-crazed province (about 250 courses), that's a drop in the bucket; secondly, he's tried to incorporate regional diversity, since several areas of the province could lay claim to all five spots by themselves.

1. **Evergreen Golf Club**. Consistently rated one of Saskatchewan's top golf courses, and for good reason, this course is nestled next to Nipawin, Tobin Lake and a huge recreational area that offers great accommodation, boating, fishing and off-roading. From the first hole – a long 600-yard par 5 carved out of the Northern forest – to scenic, rolling holes, this stunning golf course has something for every golfer – fun, challenge and exciting golf.

2. **Long Creek**. 40 minutes from Regina near Avonlea, tight fairways and ravines make this a course for target golf. Long Creek also features walks in lush meadows and thickets along a winding creek that's in play throughout many of its challenging 18 holes.

3. **Green Hills**. Located in Greenwater Provincial Park, 30 minutes from Kelvington in the east-central region, this boreal forest course features beautiful vistas and tricky shots over water. It's a good example of the more than 70 golf courses throughout Saskatchewan's network of 150 regional, provincial and national parks.

4. **Elk Ridge**. Just down the road (and outside the gates) from Prince Albert National Park's venerable Lobstick course, Elkridge features 27 holes carved out from thick forest. In this parkland setting, duffers can enjoy breathtaking views and wildlife while playing impeccably groomed, challenging holes.

5. **Mainprize**. 30 minutes southeast of Weyburn, this true links-style course rolls out undulating hills, Prairie grasses and assorted bunkers that feel like a wide-open Scottish course.

chic at Prairie prices and her Canadian design focus includes Van Gogh furniture and cast art/ceramics from the West Coast. Imports include Abbott's large hand-blown conical vases from Poland and Down the Beaten Path's extra large clay vases.

Jillian's Design Elements, 14 High St. E, (306) 693-0673, jilliansdesignelements.com

38 Renate's High Tea

The elegant rise of tea and pastry "shoppes" in cities around Canada includes Moose Jaw. If you're searching for authentic European pastries in The Jaw that weren't flown in from across the pond, look no farther than Renate's Tea Time on Main Street.

In 2006, Renate Riesch, a Liechtenstein-born pastry chef, imported her skills to this British-descended city when she opened her tea room in her husband's hometown. Her mouth-watering creations, paired with 200+ tea flavours during her High Tea, will delight any teetotallers' palate. Creamy *mille-feuille* and Bernard Callebaut chocolate *ganache* share High Tea trays with curried chicken and smoked salmon *mousse* finger sandwiches. For quality like this, Renate requires 24 hours notice for a private High Tea. She also carries a wide selection of contemporary tea pottery and china for gifts or personal indulgence.

Details: *Renate's Tea Time is open days and evenings from Easter to the end of September and open until 5:30 pm only Tuesday to Saturday from October to early April, 125B Main St. N, (306) 691-1090, renates.ca*

Copper-Clad Café 39

Moose Jaw may be known for its mineral pool and the couple dozen spas that have sprung up in the last decade, yet once you stir up a lunch appetite after a morning of personal care, it's only a short walk from most of the downtown spas to Yvette Moore's Art Gallery, which includes her Copper Café.

The stunning copper-clad interior of Yvette Moore's Gallery immediately grabs your attention in this sprawling former Land Titles Office, built in 1910.

Visitors can enjoy and purchase Ms. Moore's original and reproduction paintings ("A Canadian Prairie Artist") of recognizable Saskatchewan scenes alongside handmade gifts and home décor.

Ensconced within the gallery is the Copper Café, known for its fresh, home-cooked meals derived from regional ingredients.

The Copper Café's gastronomic experience includes innovative salads, freshly created soups and specialty breads that waft from Moose Jaw's best lunch stop.

You can also sample our most popular antioxidant in several other edible forms besides pie: saskatoon berry champagne, saskatoon berry desserts, the biggest and best saskatoon crepes and cheesecakes, saskatoon sodas and loose saskatoon berry tea that you can take home from the adjacent gift shop.

You won't be served those tiny nouvelle cuisine portions here, so bring a healthy appetite.

Details: *The gallery and café are open seven days/year-round. For the café, arrive early for lunch if you want to get a table or phone first to accommodate large groups. 76 Fairford St. W., 306-693-7600, yvettemoore.com*

40	Bookworm Festival

Every July, for three event-filled days, book lovers gather together in the scenic city of Moose Jaw to celebrate words and press the flesh with their favourite authors at the Saskatchewan Festival of Words.

The brainchild of Saskatchewan poet Gary Hyland, this popular writing event had its first planning meeting in 1996. "The Festival of Words should not exist," writes Hyland. "Located in the fourth-largest city (34,000) of a sparsely-populated hockey and bingo-loving province, a Festival that celebrates the imaginative uses of language would appear to have no raison d'etre."

Yet this vital festival does have a reason to exist: it allows the community to come together to celebrate its writers and the endangered act of reading books. If you want an insider's view of the publishing world, come and witness it first hand in this idyllic historic setting.

You'll find eager new writers excited to promote their wares, seasoned and newbie scribes sharing workshop space and literary types sipping red wine and giving each other encouragement. Best of all, for a few bucks you can sit in a hushed auditorium while a published writer reads aloud to you from their recent work.

A cultural mainstay on the Saskatchewan summer schedule, it's the highlight of the season for many sodbuster scribes and out-of-town scribblers. Past guests have included noteworthy writers like Margaret Atwood, Elizabeth Hay and *The Globe and Mail* journalist Ian Brown.

Details: *The Saskatchewan Festival of Words is held in Moose Jaw every July for three days (Fri.–Sun.). (306) 691-0557, festivalofwords.com*

We may have missed out on tectonic eruptions for mountainous terrain yet Saskatchewan has the perfect terrain for cross-country skiing: rolling terrain, coulees and if you're lucky, treed trails to wind

TAKE 5 JIM SUTHERLAND
FIVE LINKS FOR DUFFERS TO ACE

Borden-native Jim Sutherland has spent most of his adult life in Vancouver where he's worked as the editor for *Vancouver* and *Western Living* magazines and as a freelance golf writer for *enRoute*, *Westworld* and *The Globe and Mail's Report on Business* magazines. At least once a year he returns to Saskatchewan, usually in summer, for obvious reasons having to do with warmer weather and small, white, dimpled orbs.

1. **Waskesiu Golf Course in Prince Albert National Park**. Stanley Thompson was Canada's Donald Ross, Alister MacKenzie and A. W. Tillinghast, all rolled into one tempestuous package, a celebrity designer from the interwar Golden Age of Golf Design who produced no less than 16 of the country's current Top 100 courses, according to *Score Golf* magazine's annual listing. Sometimes called the Lobstick in honour of the lone tree that stands smack (and that's often the operative word) in the middle of the first fairway, Waskesiu didn't make *Score*'s cut, but it is one of the most intact of Thompson's designs and always a pleasure to play.

2. **Deer Valley, northwest of Regina**. This course, set in a deep valley a short drive northwest of Regina, keeps winning accolades for its beauty, but let's also acknowledge that it's a great test of golf. There are driving holes and target golf holes as well as some that beg to be played along the ground, especially when the wind kicks up, as it's been known to do in southern Saskatchewan. A special nod to the short par-4 8th, which involves driving up a very steep hill to a narrow landing area — a hole barely over 300 yards that yields as many sevens on the scorecard as it does threes.

through on your way to the next warming hut. Would cross-country enthusiasts be anywhere else in the middle of January?

One exceptional trail system sticks out for the skinny ski types. Just north of Duck Lake on Highway 11, Eb's Trails are the "official" trails of Saskatoon's Nordic Ski Club.

This popular trail system, which offers a challenging cross-country ski workout for every skill level, consists of 52 kilometres of groomed

3. **Borden Golf Club in Borden**. With an estimated 250 courses, Saskatchewan can probably claim more per capita than any other jurisdiction in the world — about double Scotland's ratio, for example. About 60 of them are sand-green nine-holers, a local variation that sounds quaint at best, but can be a delight to play, as is the case with this charmer a half hour's drive north-west of Saskatoon on Highway 16. Anything but a pushover, the challenging track threads through dunes and poplar bluffs, demands every shot imaginable from the hardies who play it, and is worth every penny of the $5 you'll have to stuff in the honour box.

4. **Dakota Dunes Golf Links, south of Saskatoon**. Named *Golf Digest*'s Best New Canadian Course in 2006, and currently ranked 44th in *Score Golf*'s Top 100, this dunesland beauty a few kilometres south of Saskatoon might have been even better had it been allowed to bond more completely with its site, a natural for golf. Then again, that's a quibble, and it's coming from a purist who laments the invention of earth-moving equipment. Were there an award for Best North American course charging less than $60 a round, this would surely be a candidate.

5. **Saskatchewan Landing Golf Resort at Lake Diefenbaker**. With Sageview and Harbor golf clubs, the Saskatchewan Landing Golf Resort completes one of the world's more unusual golf touring destinations. Tucked into the coulees along the gigantic reservoir created by damming the South Saskatchewan River, the trio are somewhat reminiscent of the high-desert courses of the American Southwest, but with green fees more appropriate to isolated rural areas of southwestern Saskatchewan — a winning combination in this skinflint's books.

and track-set ski trails that wind through rolling forested terrain.

Although the trail system is varied enough to allow skiers of all ages and abilities, Eb's Trails are groomed for classic skiing only. This means no skate, snowshoe or dog trails to stumble over.

Since trail maintenance and all facilities at Eb's Trails are performed by Nordic Ski Club Saskatoon volunteers, you should practice proper trail etiquette to keep these trails in shape for all users. Better yet, join this inclusive sliders' club and help out.

Then come out to enjoy Eb's Day, held every year in late February or early March, depending on the weather and snow conditions. Eb's Day was designated to recognize and honour the contributions of the trail system's namesake, Eb Fas, one of the Nordic club's long-time members.

On Eb's Day, a Sunday ski tour explores the wilderness forest, hills, valleys and frozen watersheds while keeping an eye out for those non-hibernating fauna. After the ski tour, club members, friends and families gather around a bonfire for a wiener roast and other snacks. These folks certainly know how to enjoy winter.

Details: *The trail system is accessible by two entrances, both located on the west side of Highway 11; one entrance is approximately two kilometres north of the southernmost entrance. Both entrances feature parking and a warmup hut with indoor toilet facilities. Check out current trail conditions, 306-242-1928, or visit saskatoonnordicski.ca where you can also download and print the handy Eb's Trails route map.*

42 — Twisted Trees

Like people, some trees just don't fit in with the others.

The Crooked Bush, Twisted Trees, Crooked Trees, or Crooked Trees of Alticane, is an unexplained copse of deformed aspen trees found between North Battleford and Prince Albert.

These odd trees, spread over 1.2 hectares, are a local tourist attraction that draws curious Saskatchewanians and international tourists to an isolated spot in the Redberry Lake Biosphere Reserve about 15 kilometres northwest of Hafford.

Young and not-so-young aspens are twisted in tortuous shapes. Some resemble dancers while others look like snakes. 15 metres away from the twisted trees are another copse of aspens, but those trees are oddly straight.

Biologists have been unable to

explain the phenomenon of why these trees maintain their unique stance; they continue to remain a mystery even though laboratory testing has been conducted on the soil and the trees.

Theories range from a rare genetic mutation to UFOs to even a paranormal connection.

These twisted trees are also prominent in Saskatchewan folklore. Superstitious people won't go near them under a full moon and apparently neither will wary cattle despite a lack of fencing.

It's definitely worth a Sunday drive to make your own speculations about these very strange aspens.

Details: *The "Friends of the Crooked Bush" protect the site while still allowing accessibility. The copse of crooked poplars is right by the Alticane Road, surrounded by an even gravel drive. There are boardwalks inside the copse and visitors are asked to stay on the boardwalks and away from the trees. Call (306) 549-2213 for more information.*

Beer Bottle Mountain — 43

Saskatoon needed a mountain. When the Bridge City wanted to qualify as host for the 1971 Canada Winter Games, it told Games officials: it might not be Lake Louise, but we'll make it happen.

37 kilometres south near Dundurn, Saskatchewan's first man-made ski "mountain" rose above Blackstrap Lake to a height of 90 metres with whatever was at hand at the time: beer and pop bottles, car tires and the city of Saskatoon's garbage, transported by truck.

At least that's the Prairie myth that many in Saskatchewan still recount; the official story is somewhat less romantic. A road-building contractor piled up nearly 900,000 cubic metres of rich plains soil, and by the summer of 1970, Saskatchewan had its first mountain. Dirt cheap.

Canadian Olympian-turned-Conservative Senator, Nancy Greene, anointed so-called "Beer Bottle Mountain" when she descended its thrilling 100-metre vertical for the first time in December 1970, hurtling past newly minted ski lifts, a ski jump and mature evergreen trees, frozen onto the mountain for that instant, full-grown look.

February arrived and with it the 1971 Canada Winter Games. Over the next 10 days, 40,000 spectators attended the skiing events and most days saw thousands of overflow cars parked on frozen Blackstrap Lake, monitored by nervous project engineers.

For the next 35 years, Beer Bottle Mountain became the seasonal spot where local powder heads sported their complimentary Co-op toques, Bombardier snowmobile suits and frozen blue-jeans. It was Lake Louise, Prairie-style.

At press-time for this book, Mount Blackstrap, as an operational ski and snowboard hill, is in hiatus. Owned by the Saskatchewan government, its chairlift and lodge sit unused while the decision to privatize or permanently close this Saskatchewan icon continues.

So, while area skiers and snowboarders wait for private sector saviours to return Mount Blackstrap to that nostalgic sliding hill, you can still visit the "Pimple of the Prairie" year-round, located in Blackstrap Provincial Park, or take up cross-country skiing.

Details: *Mount Blackstrap is located 30 minutes south of Saskatoon near Dundurn. Blackstrap Provincial Park also features Blackstrap Lake for wind-surfing, water skiing, sailing, fishing, swimming or hiking plus two full-service campgrounds with 50 campsites, 25 percent of them electrified. (306) 492-5675, tpcs.gov.sk.ca/Blackstrap*

44   Harmonious Heritage Park

Five clicks northeast of Saskatoon, there's a human settlement older than the Egyptian pyramids. Luckily, for those early Native peoples, there weren't any pharaohs demanding they move huge blocks of stones around.

For over 6,000 years, the nomadic tribes who roamed the Northern Plains have gathered at a certain spot to hunt bison, gather food and herbs, to seek shelter from our winter winds and to use as a place of worship and celebration. The Plains Cree called this mystical meeting place "Wanuskewin," which loosely translates as "seeking peace of mind" or "living in harmony."

Wanuskewin Heritage Park, which officially opened in June 1992, is located on the west bank of the South Saskatchewan River at the junction of Opimihaw Creek. The park is operated by a consortium of five regional Native tribes: Cree, Nakota (Sioux), Dakota (Sioux), Saulteaux (Plains Ojibwa) and Dene.

Strangely, and luckily for all Saskatchewanians, this roughly one square kilometre area was never farmed or ranched by European settlers. For some unknown reason, the previous owner left this part of the land undisturbed so it remained in pristine condition for a future national historic site to be developed.

Within its 116 hectares, you can view summer and winter camp sites, bison kill sites, tipi rings, artefacts like pottery fragments, arrowheads, animal bones and the big draw, Wanuskewin's Medicine Wheel.

The Medicine Wheel, located on a hill in the park's southwest, is estimated to be 1,500 years old. A cairn stands in the centre with an outer ring of lichen-encrusted limestone boulders and archaeologists believe the spot is where sacred ceremonies were once conducted.

Wanuskewin Heritage Park's award-winning interpretive centre absorbs over 75,000 visitors annually to begin their tour of aboriginal heritage and culture. The centre features state-of-the-art exhibits, a restaurant highlighting traditional foods, a gift shop and an art gallery.

The University of Saskatchewan manages an intensive archaeological research program at Wanuskewin and 19 separate archaeological dig sites. Some of their important finds include an 8,000-year-old spearhead, bones that have been radiocarbon-dated at 5,300 years, ancient skeletons and weapons.

Even the bison are expected to make a return. As part of a recent $10 million renewal project, the park acquired three adjacent quarter sections of land to pasture their bison herd, which had been grazing at the Wahpeton Dakota Nation.

Wanuskewin is also known for its eco-tourism opportunities. During a hike on the park's various walking trails, you can spot 184 bird species and 37 mammal species on average plus amphibians, reptiles and fish. Flora includes numerous species of trees, shrubs, grasses, sedges and herbs at the park that have been identified and interpreted for visitors.

During winter, activities include snowshoeing on the trails and ice-skating where outdoor enthusiasts can warm up with a cup of hot chocolate in the park's restaurant or sample the Bannock Bake in a traditional tipi.

Details: *Wanuskewin Heritage Park is located five kilometres north of Saskatoon on Highway 11 or take Warman Road and follow the bison icon signs. Wanuskewin is open year-round except Good Friday and between the Christmas and New Years holidays. 1-877-547-6546, 931-6767, wanuskewin.com*

Gardens of Earthly Delights   45

You might think you can grow vegetables like a pro, but maybe you haven't yet witnessed Lincoln Gardens at harvest time.

Saskatchewan's largest market garden may only have started up in the 1960s, but the tradition has been alive and well for over a hundred years in this slice of the sunny Qu'Appelle Valley.

Lincoln Gardens, like all savvy growers these days, are dedicated to ethical, sustainable agriculture. Their high quality produce is grown so that it preserves soil fertility and the majority of the field labour is done by hand, from seeding to weeding to harvesting.

This is why their largely Regina clientele are always willing to drive 15 minutes to load up with eggplant, kohlrabi, Hungarian peppers and whatever else is ready from the sizeable 53-hectare "garden."

Reginans and other visitors also gravitate to Lincoln Gardens with their own pails for the u-pick strawberries and raspberries in early July or to explore the recently developed walking trails system with those great views of the crops, valley and river.

Groups can book a spring or fall tour to Lincoln Gardens, tailored to the age group, that focuses on the life cycle of plants, a peek at the children's display garden and herb patch and to walk around this working market garden.

In the fall, Saskatchewan's largest selection of pumpkins includes 15 varieties of pumpkins in non-orange colours like the Lumina White and Australian Blue. In the Pumpkin Patch, families can be spotted picking out the perfect Halloween pumpkin, taking photos, then checking out the children's straw-bale maze and the Haunted House.

While Lincoln Gardens is the agricultural component, the Corn Maiden Garden Centre is the retail store side of the business. This independent, family-run garden centre offers bedding plants grown right on the farm, Prairie hardy perennials and shrubs, fruit trees and organic garden supplies. Corn Maiden is also an importer of fine garden and home dècor from around the world.

Upstairs from the Corn Maiden is the PookaRoola Handcraft Gallery which features unique items made by local artists and artisans as well as "fair trade" crafts from Africa, Indonesia and Mexico.

Details: *Lincoln Gardens is located on Highway 20 between Lumsden & Craven. The Country Market is open from the beginning of July through the end of October and the Corn Maiden Corn Garden Centre opens in mid-April. Please refer to the harvest schedule on their website for seasonal produce availability. (306) 731-3133, cornmaidenmarket.com*

46   The Flax Man's Flax House

When you drive into the town of Craik on Highway 11, you'll spot a long, tan-coloured building with floating brown letters along the entire west side: CRAIK FLAX HOUSE.

In 2006, entrepreneur Larry Turgeon built the Craik Flax House, a strawbale commercial property comprised almost entirely of flax, within spitting distance of Highway 11. It's all flax straw, except for several layers of coloured stucco over the bales and the roof, which was constructed from wooden trusses, metal sheeting and fibreglass insulation.

The free-standing flax structure, which provides better insulating value than Saskatchewan's traditional California stick-frame building method, is off-the-grid with a wind-powered generator and solar panels. The Flax House fits seamlessly adacent to Craik's Ecovillage, which contains an Eco-Centre and a strawbale house "subdivision."

Turgeon, a former farmer who died at 67 in January 2009, was also passionate about helping people. Instead of playing golf or watching Dr. Phil on television like other pensioners, he dedicated the rest of his life to helping people own a home by teaching them how to build with flax bales while sharing the gift of health through flax seed.

The goals of Turgeon's flax house was to create jobs using local farm products, to generate opportunities for people to work from home, which allows them more flexibility and quality time for family, and to educate people on the benefits of flax for health, comfort and affordable housing.

Known as "The Flax Man," Turgeon gently tried to sell you anything to do with locally grown golden flax seed. He sold flax straw bales for building straw bale structures (SBS) and a bevy of flax products that boasted restorative and healing properties.

Turgeon manufactured all-natural flax soap from flax oil and canola glycerine. He also sold golden flax seed oil. This miracle grain is high in omega oils, fibres and lignans that allow the body to regulate itself, improve our digestion, lower our cholesterol, blood pressure and boost our immune system.

The Flax Man promoted the health benefits of golden flax seed at home shows, trade shows and fairs across Canada.

Turgeon, who spent summers in Craik and winters in his Arizona strawbale house, even slept on a flaxseed bed that he sold from his Craik flax house. According to Turgeon, flaxseed absorbs bad chemicals within your body, relaxes muscles and always stays a constant temperature. It contains six bushels of flaxseed (about $60 worth) and he swore it would last forever — as long as it doesn't get wet.

Details: *Since Turgeon's passing, access to the Craik Flax House is limited. Contact the Town of Craik for access. (306) 734-2250, craik.ca*

Green Acres 47

In 2001, the tiny town of Craik took a radical step. The community elected to embrace a sustainability model and go green. Once a dying farm town, Craik evolved from a Highway 11 speedtrap where Roughrider fans were regularly ticketed to a gutsy green leader in rural economic development.

In just five years, Craik transformed itself from a farm town to a green community. Like many other rural Saskatchewan communities, Craik desperately needed a unique project to revitalize the dwindling community. By 2001, the town's population had declined from a peak 700 to just over 400. To maintain key services, the remaining 418 citizens knew they needed to do something drastic.

That's when environmentalist Lynn Oliphant, a retired U of S professor and head of the Prairie Institute for Human Ecology (PIHE), put forward the concept of an ecovillage — and the people of Craik ran with it.

The Craik Sustainable Living Project (CSLP) is a four-phase plan. The main goal of the CSLP is to reduce the community's ecological footprint and revitalize the town at the same time. The plan includes building an eco-centre, outreach and education, community action and the creation of an ecovillage.

An ecovillage is an urban or rural community that combines social and environmental features like sustainable living practices with community-building. Craik offered 14 residential lots for sale and in the pioneering spirit, the lots cost newcomers just $1. Phase 1 was sold out by November 2007 and the community is planning a Phase 2.

With no background in green building, the organizers needed a successful demonstration project before they could legitimately attract new settlers to Craik. In 2003–2004, they played host to a yearlong "barn-raising" and built the Eco-Centre.

The Eco-Centre is a shining example of green architecture and serves as a demonstration site for sustainable building techniques. Designed and built by green builder Cory Gordon, the 1,830-square-metre facility, which officially opened in July 2004, features an innovative and energy efficient building design and integrated heating, cooling and renewable energy systems; this includes a passive solar design, photovoltaic, a wind turbine and two ground source heat pumps.

The facility, built with post-and-beam and insulating strawbales, is comprised of 80 percent recycled materials. The timber posts and beams came from demolished grain elevators and 3,000 preserved bricks from the town's former schoolhouse live on in the Eco-Centre's Finnish-style masonry oven/fireplace.

The heating system, which works in tandem with the fireplace and roof-mounted solar panels, is in-floor radiant heating. At the entrance to the centre, a stunning solar heat retaining wall was constructed from local fieldstone and recycled cinderblocks.

In 2005, Craik received a Federation of Canadian Municipalities Sustainable Community. In 2006, the town was given a Saskatchewan Tourism Award. The accolades have created a steady stream of curious visitors (over 1,000 per year) who tour the Eco-Centre and dine at the appropriately named Solar

Garden Restaurant.

Craik also boasts a challenging nine-hole golf course with a pro shop located in the Eco-Centre. The budget-minded will enjoy the $12 green fees and, like the Eco-Centre, this golf course also uses sustainable practices. Instead of going to waste in a septic tank, the Eco-Centre's bathrooms feature composting toilets that fertilize the adjacent golf course. Just watch your step.

Details: *The Craik Ecovillage straddles the east side of Highway 11/The Louis Riel Trail, midway between Regina and Saskatoon. Open year-round. (306) 734-2242, craikecovillage.ca; Craik Golf Course: (306) 734-2364 or craik-golf@sasktel.net to reserve your tee-off time.*

48 Who Calls Valley

For those people in other provinces who believe a runaway Saskatchewan dog can still be spotted after three days, they haven't been to the Qu'Appelle Valley.

This deep topographical slice across south-central and east-central Saskatchewan, which meanders over 400 kilometres from the Manitoba boundary west into southern Saskatchewan, is our most popular southern playground. If you live in Regina, you either have a cottage in the Qu'Appelle Valley, know somebody who does or you regularly recreate in this lake-dotted getaway.

The legend of how the Qu'Appelle Valley got its name is not clear, but this explanation could be it. When North West Company fur trader Paul Harmon came to the region in 1804, Native people told him they often heard a voice crying out to them as they travelled through the valley. They called back in Cree, "Kâ-têpwêt?" ("who calls?"), or since Harmon was French-speaking, "qui appelle?"

We probably know more about how the valley was formed than the origin of the name. During the Quaternary Period, about 14,000 years ago, Saskatchewan was covered on four occasions by glaciers.

When these glaciers melted, they created so much meltwater that they eroded the water channel that eventually became the Qu'Appelle Valley. Each time the glaciers melted, material trapped within the ice was deposited along the earth's surface.

After the last glacier melted, the Qu'Appelle Valley was entirely filled with water. As the land continued to shift, the four lakes we have today became shallower as they accumulated alluvium (soil or sediments deposited by a river or other running water) and gravel from numerous landslides.

Echo, Katepwa, Mission and Pasqua, known collectively as the Calling Lakes, are fed by the Qu'Appelle River and even deeper aquifers beneath them. These four bodies of water, ringed by an undulating valley, provide natural beauty and a plethora of recreational and cultural opportunities, from watersports to camping to food and arts tourism.

If you're ever been called to the Qu'Appelle Valley, you'll know it's for a good time.

Details: *Check out sasktourism.com for more recreational info in the Qu'Appelle Valley or 1-877-2ESCAPE (1-877-237-2273).*

Cherries on the Prairies 49

Dean and Sylvia Kreutzer might have always been fruit lovers, but they didn't necessarily have the experience to grow fruit-bearing tress. But why let a little thing like inexperience get in the way of developing a commercial cherry orchard on the Prairies?

The Kreutzers wanted to produce a popular tourist and organic fruit production area in Saskatchewan. So, in 2000, they pulled up their mini-orchard in their Regina yard and transplanted them in the beginnings of a 10-hectare orchard 20 minutes northwest of the city.

Now these savvy fruit growers stage guided tours of their orchard and retail a bevy of packaged products from the fruit of their labours, including chocolate-covered cherries and fruit spreads.

This is no U-pick. The Kreutzers will take you on a personal tour of the Over the Hill orchards where you can see the direct benefits of their innovative — and certified organic — Prairie fruit operations. The Kreutzers grow four hectares of sour cherries and six hectares of plums, apples and apricots.

They also offer two types of tours from May to the end of August.

Orchard Tour #1 is a group walking tour (a minimum of 10) of the four-hectare sour cherry orchard, which includes a discussion of the different cherry varieties, organic methods, the importance of bees and the pollination process and what happens at harvest time. The cherry orchard's blooming period is in mid-May and the cherry harvest is during the end of July.

The tour also includes the unique growing methods for growing exotic fruits such as strawberries, blueberries, peaches, apricots, blackberries, greenhouse growing and a discussion on fruit breeding.

They grow all six varieties of cherries that the University of Saskatchewan's Bob Bors and Rick Sawatsky developed for our growing conditions. The Carmin Jewel series is the only cherry variety currently producing fruit, which the Kreutzers have branded the "Prairie Cherry."

Tour #2 is the orchard tour plus a short yet scenic drive to nearby Lumsden where the lucky folks who paid a few extra dollars get a delicious slice of Prairie Cherry pie served with organic coffee at the Prairie Cherry Corner retail location.

It's only $6/person for Tour #1 and 1-1.5 hours of your day and $10/person for their two-hour Tour #2.

The retail store in Lumsden is where visitors can also scoop up their certified organic Prairie cherry products such as the very popular chocolate-covered Prairie Cherry Delights.

Other succulent packaged products from Over the Hill Orchards include cherry, saskatoon, raspberry and blueberry spreads and pies that include apple, or the Prairie Rainbow (cherries, apples, rhubarb, saskatoons, raspberries) with an organic spelt flour crust.

Details: *The orchard operation is 20 minutes northwest of Regina. Detailed driving instructions for tours will be emailed or mailed to tour participants with a confirmation and invoice. Over the Hill's retail store, Prairie Cherry Corner, in nearby Lumsden sells their products plus it offers a brunch and dessert menu. Orchard: (306) 530-9133; Lumsden Store: 20A Second Avenue, (306) 731-1442, overthehillorchards.ca*

50 Inspired Grub

There are only two types of food in Saskatchewan: inspired and uninspired. The New Ground Café in Birch Hills (pop. 1,000), 37 kilometres south of Prince Albert, definitely falls into the inspired category with its focus on slow food.

Located on Birch Hill's downtown commercial strip, New Ground's chef-owner Jennifer Willems has stirred the pot of rural Saskatchewan cuisine since opening in December 2005.

When you walk into this unpretentious noshery, the first three things you notice are the alluring kitchen aroma, the original artwork and a red 1940s sofa with an inviting slogan "Sit long, talk much, laugh often" inscribed above it.

To the affable and dynamic Willems, comfort food is poverty cuisine. She believes in using what you have on hand, making due with less and stretching your protein. The New Ground's motto is "local ingredients, global flavour." Her twist is substituting a local ingredient for a non-local ingredient and often adding some global influence to a traditional comfort food.

Originally from north of La Ronge, Willems and her family grew up in the bush without television, so she took an interest in food creation early. This self-taught chef is certainly on the right track with her food philosophy and her contribution to Saskatchewan's new culinary direction.

Willems incorporates foods from Northern Saskatchewan with Prairie ingredients to create hearty menu items that celebrate her Métis heritage and the bounty of local foods: Golden Flax Bannock, Red River Cinnamon Buns, Bison Nachos, Birch Syrup Cappuccinos and Chokecherry Chai Vinaigrette are paired with inspired soups, other freshly made baked good and fair trade organic coffee.

Willems recycles her organic coffee grounds into her chocolate cheesecake and as a sprinkle for the home-made cinnamon buns. Survivors of the "Dirty Thirties" would approve of her culinary thrift and urbanites will enjoy the exotic variety and country prices.

The townspeople thought Willems was "weird" when she and her carpenter husband first opened a 14-seat diner down the street. When they bought and renovated their present brick building that once housed a pharmacy for 70 years, then a greasy spoon, they managed to usurp the former diner's overactive deep fryer.

Now most of the townies have come around to this local foodie's philosophy. So have customers who regularly drive from nearby Melfort and Prince Albert with an appetite and an open mind for New Ground's innovative and inexpensive dishes.

Willems has also been noticed internationally. This slow food advocate was invited to the 2008 Slow Food Terra Madre in Turin, Italy where she was able to share ideas and recipes with other enthusiasts.

New Ground also offers on- and off-piste catering, private bookings, monthly live music events and a weekly farmer's market, June–September.

Details: *The New Ground Café is open on weekdays only for coffee or lunch, 9:30 am – 4 pm and for dinner (reservations required) on Thursday until 9 pm. Get on the email list to be notified of monthly dinner/live music events. 167 Bellamy Avenue, Birch Hills, (306) 749-2529, newground@sasktel.net*

The Wheat Wizard of Rosthern — 51

There are boy wizards like Harry Potter and then there are Saskatchewan wheat wizards. Seager Wheeler, the Wheat Wizard of Rosthern who won five World Wheat Championships, is easily the Prairie provinces' most famous farmer. Seager Wheeler's 75-hectare Maple Farm was even designated a National Historic Site in 1996.

Born in England (1868-1961), Seager Wheeler emigrated to what is now Saskatchewan in 1885 and after various city jobs, homesteaded in 1890 east of what is now Rosthern.

Once Wheeler, a newbie farmer, educated himself in the principles of dry land farming, he applied his new skills by entering prize-winning produce at local fairs. In 1911, he sent a grain crop sample to the New York Land Show and won the $1,000 first prize in gold coins for the best hard spring wheat grown in North America. Between 1915 and 1918, he picked up four more wheat awards for competitions around North America.

Wheeler was the author of numerous publications on progressive farming techniques, including "Profitable Grain Growing" in 1919, a best-selling study of dry-land farming and the most comprehensive compilation of scientific agricultural techniques at that time.

Wheeler also gained renown as a farm implements inventor and as the developer of new grain and horticultural varieties including several types of wheat, barley and even fruit trees that will survive in our harsh climate. Scientists, universities and farmers on three continents requested seed samples from the Wheat Wizard.

Wheeler became a prominent educator in this new scientific agriculture and Queens University in Kingston conferred him with an honourable degree in 1920. In 1943, King George VI admitted Wheeler as a Member of the Order of the British Empire.

Stop in where it all started. Maple Grove Farm, including many original buildings, has been restored to its 1919 operating condition and, just as Dr. Seager Wheeler would have preferred, this is not an idle place. This innovative farm continues to be an integral part of agricultural research and demonstration.

Wheeler's farm wasn't just about grain. He also developed an impressive English flower garden and an orchard that was once the largest on the Prairies; it's now being restored and replanted.

Wheeler's philosophy was all about how agriculture and nature can co-exist. Birdwatchers can witness this in the 24-hectare bird sanctuary and marsh.

Visitors can also check out the gift shop, stop for tea and pie in Wheeler's century old house or attend seasonal events such as the Spring Orchard Seminar and Pruning Day, Mother's Day Buffet, English High Teas, Children's Day Camps, Fruit Festival or the Harvest Supper.

Details: *The Seager Wheeler Farm National Historic Site is open from early May to early September, 9 am – 5 pm. Closed Mondays. From Rosthern (Highway 11), drive east on Highway 312 for seven kilometres, then .5 kilometre north on the grid road. (306) 232-5959, seagerwheelerfarm.org*

52 Thick With Artists

Ladies, it's finally time to get revenge on your husband for that protracted hockey play-off season every spring or for hiding in his basement workshop carving a mallard duck instead of mowing the lawn.

At any rate, summertime is the perfect excuse to assert your will, demand some pay back and insist he and the kids now accompany you on a lengthy tour of artisans' studios in rural Saskatchewan.

For one weekend in early August, the Shell Lake area plays host to an annual Thickwood Hills Studio Trail that will satisfy every curious collector in search of home-grown Saskatchewan-made art to grace the living room. Potters and painters, blacksmiths and weavers, sculptors and carvers are all poised in their open studios working away and eager to greet you.

If you can't find a Thickwood Hills Studio Trail brochure at a tourism information office, you can surf the web to map the best route. If you follow the blue moon signs, they'll lead you to 18 studio stops along this marathon artisans' route. It may not equal seven months of hockey, but it's a good start.

Details: *Studios are open 10 am – 9 pm or by appointment. Thickwood Hills Studio Trail, Shell Lake, (306) 427-2178, studiotrail.com*

Purple Teeth by the River 53

One of our favourite summer rituals in Saskatchewan is saskatoon berry picking. Ice cream pail in hand, you gather them with one hand and add them to the pail with the other — stuffing a few berries into your mouth until you're satisfied.

The next best thing to spotting a loaded clump of ripe saskatoon berry bushes next to the roadside on a hot July day is a visit to The Berry Barn, who luckily provide a U-pick just ten minutes south of Saskatoon.

This family-owned orchard and restaurant, "The Berry Barn Eatery," is managed and operated by Ed and Darlene Derdal, daughter Natalie and her husband Grant Erlandson. Even the grandkids lend a hand.

The Derdal's 11-hectare orchard operation produces over 10,000 kilograms at harvest time in June–July. The family also operates a greenhouse with bedding plants and locally-grown vegetables.

The Berry Barn Eatery looks out onto the scenic South Saskatchewan River. Ask for a table on their busy deck for the best view. If you have a sweet tooth, you can order orchard-fresh saskatoon berry pie, sundaes, teas, ciders, chocolates and fudge. They also offer a full menu for those hearty eaters who want more than just dessert.

If you're in the market for a unique wedding locale, the Derdals have created a romantic little oasis in their berry orchard, complete with quaint gazebo where you can tie the knot then seal the deal with a slice of saskatoon berry pie.

Details: *The Berry Barn is located at 830 Valley Road, 11 kilometres south of Saskatoon, just before Highway 60. Open seven days during the summer, 10 am – 8 pm. Restaurant reservations are recommended. Call or surf first to confirm their days and hours of operation. (306) 978-9797, theberrybarn.com*

54 Last Stand at Batoche

The 1885 Northwest Rebellion might only be a memory blip from history class for most Canadians; in Saskatchewan, it's common knowledge.

If you prefer to linger and imagine the scent of long ago saddle leather and gunpowder, Batoche is for you. Batoche is where the final battle of the Northwest Rebellion was fought, an 88 kilometre jaunt north-east of Saskatoon. Of course, who won and who lost is now a moot point. Canada, a young country at the time, was merely experiencing "growing pains."

Located in the South Saskatchewan River Valley, Batoche was the headquarters of Métis leader Louis Riel's short-lived Provisional Government of Saskatchewan. This is where Canada's first and only "civil war" was ultimately decided through violent action.

Opened in 1923, the Batoche National Historic Site of Canada portrays Métis culture and heritage from 1860 to 1900. The impressive Visitor Reception Centre houses a theatre that depicts the story of the 1885 uprising in an award-winning 42-minute multi-media presentation plus a bevy of artefacts, Métis and non-Métis.

The 365-hectare site is broken into four areas, and if you go, you'll need at least a good four hours to adequately absorb Batoche and its history.

A ten-minute walk across an open field from the entrance leads to the only original structures, a stunning white Catholic church and rectory, both built in the early 1880s. Bullet holes are visible in the rectory walls from the Battle of Batoche where, out-numbered and short of ammunition, the Métis surrendered on May 12 after only four days.

The rebellion's final clash involved less than 300 lightly-armed Métis in rifle pits against General Middleton's 800 North West Field Force members and several cannons.

Batoche's landscape consists of undulating parkland with brush-filled sections, perfect for Métis rifle pits. Riel's military leader, Gabriel Dumont, escaped after the battle and joined Buffalo Bill Cody's Wild West Show in the U.S. for a few years.

The Prime Minister on our ten-dollar bill gave the Métis fighters amnesty in 1886 and Dumont eventually returned to the area. This dynamic yet elusive Métis leader is now safely buried under a sizeable stone in the church cemetery.

If you're keen to see another Northwest Rebellion battleground, drive 30 kilometres south to The Battle of Fish Creek National Historic Site which commemorates the April 24, 1885 skirmish that delayed the Battle of Batoche.

Details: *The Batoche National Historic Site is located 88 kilometres northeast of Saskatoon on Highway 225. Open daily 9 am – 5 pm, May 8–September 30. The Fish Creek Battlefield site is 15 kilometres south of Highway 312 at the Highway 225/312 junction to Batoche. Watch for the Parks Canada beaver icon signs to both sites. (306) 423-6227, parkscanada.ca*

Fort Fur Trade 55

Imagine the Hudson's Bay Company (HBC) before store mannequins, perfume counters and long line-ups to return unwanted Christmas gifts on Boxing Day.

The old school HBC was based around the fur trade and its rugged employees didn't wear nametags or probably take time to bathe regularly. Luckily we live in different times.

Straight west of Batoche and 110 kilometres north of Saskatoon is HBC Fort Carlton. Situated on a flat plain beside the North Saskatchewan River, this HBC post, built in 1810 and operated until 1885, was the most active fur-trading hub in the region.

Although not a NWMP fort, HBC's Fort Carlton was still caught in the crossfire during the 1885 Northwest Rebellion. Abandoned by its employees, it was subsequently looted and burned by Métis and Natives.

The reconstructed fort includes the palisade, stores for fur, provisions and trade plus a clerk's quarters. Just don't expect any ongoing 30-percent-off sales on trendy clothes, pillow-top queen beds or clacking escalators in this HBC store. Instead, you can see, touch and smell artefacts like buffalo hides, beaver pelts, war clubs, blankets, guns, twist tobacco and birch bark baskets.

You'll also find knowledgeable, interactive staff that will guide you through these special areas of interest. They'll answer your questions plus lead you in activities like playing the spoons or packing furs for the long trip to England.

Outside the palisade walls stands a tipi encampment and the remnants of the old Carlton Trail are still visible from the deep ruts left by Red River carts.

In-park services include a gift shop, a visitor centre and displays. A sheltered picnic area, primitive camping (no services) and group camping are also available.

The River Walk is a short path from the fort gates to the South Saskatchewan River where hardy boatmen and freighters once used 25-foot canoes and York boats to haul their goods. During the summer months, groups of Saskatoon canoeists regularly dock at Fort Carlton and help keep this remnant of early Saskatchewan history alive.

Details: *Fort Carlton Provincial Park is 110 kilometres north of Saskatoon. Take Highway 11 to Duck Lake then drive west on Highway 212. The route is well-marked. Open 10 am – 6 pm Victoria Day weekend to Labour Day weekend. Phone or email first about camping rates and availability. (306) 467-5205, FortCarlton@gov.sk.ca, tpcs.gov.sk.ca/FortCarlton*

South

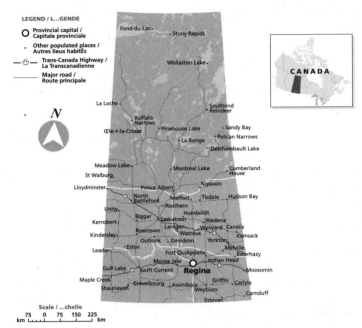

N

CANADA

Scale / ...chelle
75 0 75 150 225
km ⌞⌟⌟⌟⌟⌟⌟   ⌟ km

56   Hot on the Outlaw Trail

In the south-central Big Muddy Bad-lands, temperatures often rise to a sti-fling 35 degrees and only the deer, antelope and cacti are really at home on the range.

Visitors to this remote area, a two-hour drive from Regina near the Montana border, are treated to stunning scenery, an abundance of wildlife and rich history from a little-known part of Saskatchewan.

The Big Muddy Badlands is not only cattle country. At the turn of the last century, it was also outlaw territory. The glacier-tilled land-scape — caves carved from the sandstone by wind and water and winding, treed coulees surrounded by arid, undulating land — was sparsely populated and lightly policed. From the 1880s to the early 1900s, many American outlaws used the Big Muddy as a base to rob banks and trains or steal horses in Montana. Outlaws fleeing American justice only had to make a short horseback ride across the border. Some expanded their crimes into Canada.

When lawmen finally moved into Valley County in Montana, outlaws such as Dutch Henry and his brother Coyote Pete, Sam Kelly and the Pigeon Toed Kid, among others, moved into the Big Muddy. The notorious Sundance Kid also turned up in the area.

Although it's possible to visit the region on your own, the best way to explore the Big Muddy is with a guided tour provided by the Coronach Tourism Board's three knowledgeable guides. Also, because many of the most interesting Big Muddy spots are on private ranch land, travelling with one of the guides is the best — and only legal — way in. (A sign on one rancher's gate along the tour threatens "Trespassers will be given a fair trial then hung!")

The engaging six-hour tour covers up to 170 kilometres and includes lessons in geology, ornithology, botany, anthropology and history. Once you've left Coronach, you'll soon see Castle Butte, an Ice Age relic, looming in the valley below. You can put your hiking shoes to work and climb the 60-metre peak for a better view of the three-kilometre wide valley.

The next memorable stop is the village of Big Beaver, where Aust's General Store, a family-owned enterprise built in the late 1920s, proudly proclaims: "If we don't have it, you don't need it."

Next up is the Burgess Ranch, which covers more than 8,000 hectares and is one of four private ranches included on the tour. While you eat your brown-bag lunch, rancher Tammy Burgess, an artist and writer, shares stories about the outlaws of the Big Muddy. The Burgess Ranch buildings sit almost exactly where the North West Mounted Police escorted Sitting Bull and his band of Sioux back to the United States in 1881; they had sought sanctuary in Canada after the 1876 massacre of U.S. Cavalry troops at Little Bighorn, Montana.

After lunch, it's time for a visit to the remains of the Big Muddy NWMP Post before heading to the Sam Kelly Outlaw Caves. Outlaws used the sandstone caves, carved into the hills from smaller existing caves, to hide from lawmen and posses in hot pursuit. One smaller, lower cave was used to shelter several outlaws while a larger cave up the hill was used to hide up to six stolen horses in a shaft almost 10 metres deep.

The shelter has been reduced in size after several cave-ins, but the names and dates of outlaws waiting for posses to pass are etched into the hard sandstone. From the hills above the caves you'll have a stunning view of the Big Muddy region. Just across the valley, the Big Muddy Badlands' short-grass Prairie undulates south into Montana.

Details: *Guided tours are available through Coronach's tourism board from early June to early September. Tours, lasting three or six hours, must be booked in advance. Coronach hosts its annual Outlaw Days Festival in late July. (306) 267-3312, bigmuddybadlands.com*

The Finnish Noah   57

Back in Noah's time, building your own boat was probably a good idea. We know how that turned out for him.

In the 1930s and early 1940s, Finnish immigrant Tom Sukanen, who homesteaded near the south-central communities of Macrorie and

Birsay, wanted to build an ocean-going ship. Although he now lived in a landlocked province, he still had delusions of sailing his craft down the South Saskatchewan River and back to Finland. His neighbours didn't recognize Sukanen as another Noah in their midst. Unlike Noah, Sukanen's story took a tragic turn.

Born Tomi Jannus Alankola on September 23, 1878, he learned the shipbuilding trade in his teens. Alankola was able to read a sextant and a compass — two very important tools for ocean navigation.

In 1898, Alankola was a sturdy, 200-pound 20-year-old. Like thousands of other young men from Finland, he set sail for America. He intended to use his ship building knowledge, especially with steel, to work then return to his homeland and live comfortably. After an unsuccessful job hunt, he ended up in Minnesota where he started farming.

Now known as Tom Sukanen, he met a young woman, also a Finn, and fathered four children. By 1911, Sukanen decided to head for Canada on foot in search of a brother who was farming in the Macrorie-Birsay area. He planned to secure a homestead and bring his family to live in Canada.

In 1916, Sukanen walked the same 1,000 kilometres back to his former home in Minnesota. He soon learned his wife had died in a flu epidemic and his son and three daughters had been placed into foster homes by authorities. He tried twice unsuccessfully to rescue his son and Sukanen was deported.

In 1929, Sukanen took a heavy rowboat to the spring high waters of the South Saskatchewan River and he navigated waterways all the way to Hudson Bay. He then took a job on a freighter and found his way home to Finland. This was Sukanen's trial run. Before his departure, he secured a complete set of maps from the Regina Department of Archives to plan his route for when he could navigate a larger ship back to his home country.

Soon after Sukanen returned to the Birsay-Marcrorie area in the early 1930s from Finland, a sizeable shipment of steel, sheet metal, cable and copper arrived at the Macrorie rail station. These were the materials Sukanen would use to fulfill his shipbuilding dream. Now the community realized that he was serious about building a large boat and returning to Finland. Day and night his neighbours could see the glow of his forge or hear the pounding of his heavy hammers

TAKE 5 — TREVOR HERRIOT
A BIRDER'S MUST LIST

Trevor Herriot (trevorherriot.com) is a Prairie naturalist, illustrator, writer and a regular guest on CBC Saskatchewan's mid-day Radio One program, *Blue Sky*, where he answers questions on birds. His three non-fiction books, *River in a Dry Land*, *Jacob's Wound*, and, most recently, *Grass, Sky, Song* for HarperCollins, have received national attention. Trevor and his wife, Karen, have four children and divide their time between Regina and their cottage.

1. **Chaplin Lake**. One of the best shorebirding spots on the continent, Chaplin Lake hosts more than 30 species of shorebirds, some of them numbering in the tens of thousands during migration. My favourite time to go is in late May or mid-August when I can watch massive flocks of sanderlings and other sandpipers turn and wheel in unison — and sometimes peregrine falcons in hot pursuit. In summer, it's one of the easiest places to spot the endangered piping plover.

2. **Prince Albert National Park**. For the birds of the great boreal wilderness, you can do no better than this park. It offers almost 4,000 square kilometres of habitat and a couple hundred bird species that include 20 or more wood warblers. I like to hang out at the Narrows' day use area, watching loons and other water birds, then go for a long slow walk at nearby Treebeard nature trail on the lookout for warblers and five species of woodpeckers.

to bind and rivet the steel portions of the ship and to shape the ship's boiler.

Like a Finnish Noah preparing for a predicted flood whispered into his ear by God, Sukanen kept at his mission, stopping for only a few hours of sleep each night. His farm stood neglected. By early 1943, the ten-metre ship, christened the *Sontiainen*, was ready. Just a couple of problems: no money to transport it to the South Saskatchewan River and Sukanen was arrested by the RCMP who claimed he posed a threat to both himself and the community. Sukanen was transported to the mental institution near North Battleford where he died on April 23, 1943, age 64.

As for Tom's ship, it's still in the province. Sukanen's sizeable craft,

3. Roche Percée. Here's a birding hotspot you'll have all to yourself. Not a national or provincial park, Roche Percée is a small recreational and historic site 22 kilometres south of Estevan. It attracts a good mix of Saskatchewan's aspen parkland and valley songbirds and birds whose primary range is farther to the south and east: field sparrow, yellow-throated vireo, eastern wood-pewee, eastern screech owl and eastern bluebird. Roche Percée is of the best spots to find both rose-breasted and black-headed grosbeaks.

4. Grasslands National Park. There are many good reasons to go to this park; Prairie birdlife is one of them. Most of Canada's increasingly rare grassland birds can be seen either in the park or along roads that go through ranchland adjacent to the park: burrowing owl, greater sage-grouse (requires some luck), ferruginous hawk, long-billed curlew, Sprague's pipit, sage thrasher, loggerhead shrike, Brewer's sparrow, Baird's sparrow, McCown's longspur, chestnut-collared longspur and many more.

5. Cypress Hills Interprovincial Park. This cross-boundary park is a bit of the Rocky Mountains' foothills that reach east onto the plains. Western and montane species breed here and nowhere else in Saskatchewan, including dusky flycatcher, red-naped sapsucker, MacGillivray's warbler, pink-sided junco, and Audubon's yellow-rumped warbler. Be sure to explore the hiking trails of the park's West Block in and around Fort Walsh.

which never saw water — fresh or salt — is now part of an early 20th century Prairie village within a museum named for this scrappy Finn. It proudly anchors The Sukanen Ship Pioneer Village Museum, 13 kilometres south of Moose Jaw where it was moved in 1973 from its original location. The *Sontiainen*, restored by local volunteers, was officially dedicated on June 19, 1977 to "all the pioneers who had done so much to ensure the future of us all."

The museum grounds are also home to a piece of history connected to an equally determined yet better-known Prairie pioneer, John Diefenbaker. The Diefenbaker homestead, originally from the Borden district, was moved in 2005 from its previous stop in Regina's Wascana Centre.

Details: *Sukanen's ship is beached 13 kilometres south of Moose Jaw on Highway 2. The Sukanen Ship Pioneer Village Museum is open daily from mid-May to the third week of September then weekends only until freeze up. (306) 693-7315, sukanenmuseum.ca*

58 Grasslands Sanctuary

Do you prefer tree-free national parks because they get in the way of a good view? Then our second national park, Grasslands, is for you.

First agreed-upon in 1981 by federal and provincial parties yet not officially opened until 2001, Grasslands National Park is the only one of 39 national parks to preserve a portion of the mixed Prairie grasslands. This 906-square-kilometre park is just one part of a larger Canadian system of protected heritage areas where the goal is to protect representations of each of Canada's 39 natural regions. In less than a century, our Prairie grasslands became one of the most endangered habitats in the country.

If you love the subtle nature and space of the Prairie landscape, this is the place where flora and fauna aren't just Siamese twins on the Addams Family. Grasslands Park's low-impact, cardiovascular activities include guided hikes, interpretive trails, bird watching and nature photography.

The park promotes habitat restoration and species preservation and reintroduction. Through the joint efforts of committed Prairie conservationists, an astounding range of common and endangered Prairie flora and fauna still exist. Easy to spot flora includes blue gramma grass, historically a favourite of the bison herds that once grazed through here, needle-and-thread grass, the delicate purple-pink flowers of Bessey's Locoweed, prickly pear cactus that breathes only at night and gumbo evening primrose, that quirky flower who can't make up its mind so it changes colour every 24 hours.

While our ancestors may have found cheap land to homestead upon, they quickly displaced and even eradicated fauna such as bison, Prairie wolf, Plains grizzly, elk, wolverine, swift fox and black-footed ferret. As for Gainer the Gopher's endangered relatives, the black-tailed Prairie dog, these busy rodents can now only be found in colonies in and around the park but no where else in Canada. You should be able to spot Prairie-adapted common and endangered species like the pronghorn antelope, sage grouse, burrowing owl, ferruginous hawk, eastern short-horned lizard and even the Prairie rattlesnake — or perhaps you don't.

After 120 years of absence, those linebackers of Team Grasslands, the Plains bison, were re-introduced into Grasslands National Park in December 2005. The initial herd, which consisted of 71 bison, arrived from Elk Island National Park and their range area now totals approximately 181 square kilometres.

The stunning landscape can't be forgotten. The Frenchman River Valley in the park's West Block is a result of a glacial meltwater channel that features deeply dissected plateaus, coulees and the landmark 70-mile Butte. If you want to view the surrounding countryside, you'll have to work for it with a hike. The park's East Block features the Killdeer "Badlands" of the Rock Creek area where the first recorded dinosaur remains in Western Canada were discovered in 1874.

Details: *The Visitor Reception Centre in Val Marie is open daily, Victoria Day weekend to Labour Day, then weekdays only to March 31. Two new campgrounds will be installed for 2010. Limited openings. Phone ahead. The park is always open. (306) 298-2257, parkscanada.ca*

Hurry Hard to the Turner 59

Imagine you're so keen on curling that you filled your basement with curling paraphernalia — then invited strangers to come and peruse your hobby.

When Don and Elva Turner of Weyburn, both avid curlers, first started a curling museum in the basement of their home in the late 1960s, it was the first and only major museum in the world dedicated exclusively to curling. It still is. In November 1990, when their extensive collection outgrew their re-modelled basement, the Turners moved the museum to a 800-square-metre building attached to the Weyburn Leisure Centre.

The Turner Curling Museum protects and preserves the history and artefacts of this celebrated — and official — Saskatchewan sport. In 2001, the Saskatchewan legislature adopted curling as the province's official sport in recognition of its provincial significance plus the international contribution of Saskatchewan curlers to the sport. Weyburn's curling museum attracts visitors from as far away as Scotland, curling's birthplace.

Curling has always played a central role in Saskatchewan recreation and sport. The first recorded game of curling in Saskatchewan was played on the North Saskatchewan River in Prince Albert on January 17, 1882. Players used blocks of wood cut from tamarack trees as curling stones.

The Turner Curling Museum contains the largest collection of curling memorabilia anywhere in the world — and it's still growing: 18,000 curling pins, 200 crests, 300 curling books, 200 photos of rinks, 75 curling stones (ranging in weight from eight to 30 kilograms), a variety of brooms, sweaters, tams, plus any other paraphernalia even closely related to our official sport. The Turners also collected some very unusual curling items such as curling irons made from melted cannonballs that date from the 1760s, sterling silver handles (apparently never put into action) and an 1898 New York City curling pin (a prize from a curling bonspiel) found in a time capsule inside a Regina house.

The Turner Curling Museum also stocks a large collection of pins for sale and this non-profit organization still accepts items for display. So if you're a curling nut or just a curious spectator, make sure you "hurry hard" to Weyburn to experience this shrine to our favourite winter pastime.

Details: *The Turner Curling Museum is open Saturday and Sunday 2–5 pm year-round. Limited wheelchair accessibility and special tours can be arranged. Admission is free but donations are gratefully accepted. 530 – 5th St. NE, Weyburn. (306) 848-3283*

60   Saskatchewan's Silverado

Weyburn contains the largest known collection of curling memorabilia with its Turner Curling Museum. Yet this collection-crazy city of

10,000 is also home to the largest one-man collection of silver.

Saskatchewan's "silverado," located inside Weyburn's Soo Line Historical Museum, houses the Charles Wilson Silver Collection, the largest one-man collection of silver known to exist anywhere — and the museum's feature attraction. While some Prairie people collect matchbooks in used pickled egg jars from every motel and greasy spoon they ever darkened, old Charlie really liked his silver. His size-able — and valuable — collection of silver consists of over 3,300 items. When this local bachelor wasn't farming, he was collecting silver from auctions, estate sales and antique shops around North America and Europe. He even convinced auction houses to bid for him when he wasn't able to attend.

The Charles Wilson Silver Collection is an astounding and comprehensive collection that covers several generations of his own family and apparently other families, too. The collection's major groups feature salt and pepper shakers, tea service sets and cream and sugar sets. Trays, platters, pictures, spoons and figurines are also visible in large glass display cases.

It's not all about silver. There are actually 5,000 varied items from Charlie Wilson's farmhouse, dating from 1750 to 1972, and all bequeathed to the Soo Line Historical Museum when he died at age 91 in 1995. Some of the collection encompasses the Art Nouveau style and Victorian era: items can be grouped into categories of china, cut glass, Bohemian and Pinwheel crystal. Furniture and other antiques from Mr. Wilson's lifetime of gathering round out the collection.

Besides Charlie Wilson's valuable personal items, the museum also features Weyburn and district pioneer artefacts displayed by theme. One strange artefact that once belonged to Mr. Wilson in the "Farm" room is worth the price of admission: an eight-legged calf — six appendages on the bottom and two protruding from its back — stands immortalized by a professional taxidermist. This bovine oddity was found in Mr. Wilson's bedroom after he died. Charlie, a sworn bachelor, obviously didn't have a wife to discourage his eccentric décor choices.

Details: *The Soo Line Historical Museum is located on Highway 39 in the circa 1909 brown brick building (a former power plant) with the huge smoke stack. Open year-round. Admission: $5 adults and seniors; $4 youth; $2 children. (306) 842-2922, silver.sasktelwebsite.net*

Meet Me At Roche Percée | 61

Not just teenagers get piercings. So do rocks.

Roche Percée or "pierced rock" is a grouping of rocks situated southeast of Estevan near the Saskatchwan-North Dakota border. This 1.3 hectare oddity, now part of La Roche Percée Provincial Historic Site, straddles the village of Roche Percée (pop. 162) in the Souris River Valley.

The stone structures at Roche Percée weren't placed there by aliens or Stonehenge druids. Actually, this large sandstone outcrop was formed into unusual shapes by the forces of erosion. Water originally flowed through swamps where plant remains accumulated to form Saskatchewan's lignite/coal deposits. When the exposed lignite eventually became sandstone, it was rapidly eroded by wind and water.

The Nakota Sioux's name for the sandstone outcropping was translated by Métis that travelled through the region into "La Roche Percée." The rock was once completely covered with pre-contact petroglyph carvings of human, animal and geometric forms, inscribed into the soft sandstone. The Nakota considered the site to be sacred; they never passed the rock without leaving an offering.

The North West Mounted Police made their first major camp here during their initial 1874 trek westward and a stone cairn commemorates the Short Creek Camp. Even members of Custer's ill-fated U.S. 7th Cavalry are rumoured to have visited our pierced rocks.

La Roche Percée became a popular sightseeing spot for area settlers who carved their names and initials into this significant landmark. Although legally protected, visitors still can't resist pulling out a scraping tool to leave their personal mark on this unique, pierced sandstone.

Details: *La Roche Percée Provincial Historic Site & Short Creek Cairn is located approximately 20 kilometres southeast of Estevan, just off Highway 39 and adjacent to the CPR's Soo Line. The site is open year-round but it's definitely more accessible from spring until fall. Free admission. (306) 577-2600, southeast.sask.info*

62 The Real Prairie Giant

Saskatchewan may have born a few political and sports giants since becoming a province in 1905. But real giants weigh 370 pounds, stand above the crowd at 8' 3" and are soon courted by a large American circus as a side-show act.

Saskatchewan's giant, Joseph Edouard Beaupré, was born on January 9, 1881 in the small French and Métis community of Willow Bunch south of Moose Jaw. One of Saskatchewan's oldest settlements, Willow Bunch was first settled in 1870 by wintering Métis hunters from Manitoba.

Beaupré, the eldest son of French-Canadian father Gaspard

Beaupré, 5′ 8″, and Métis mother Florestine Piché, 5′ 4″, only weighed nine pounds at birth and apparently he seemed normal — until he turned three years old. Beaupré suddenly started to grow like a Saskatchewan weed. A benign tumor, unknown to anybody until his death, had attached to his pituitary gland, which determines the body's growth, and up he shot. At nine, he measured 6′. At 12, 6′ 6″ and at 17 when he lifted an 800-pound horse, Beaupré stood 7′ 1″.

Beaupré travelled to Montana where he worked on a ranch to realize a dream of becoming a cowboy. But his height and weight got in his way since horses that large are hard to find. While in Montana, he met an American that convinced him to join the circus for a living and that's when Beaupré, now 21, measured 7′ 11″ and weighed 365 pounds. His neck measured 21 inches, his chest 56 inches and his shoes, size 22, were special ordered.

Beaupré travelled throughout North America with circus shows that exhibited his extraordinary stature and strength. From 1898 to 1904, he earned a living being ogled, wrestling strongmen and performing feats of strength. One of his most popular stunts was crouching beneath an 800-pound horse then lifting it to shoulder height.

Promoters tried unsuccessfully to marry Beaupré to the tallest woman in the world, Miss Ella Ewing, a giantess who stood 7′ 6″ because he showed no interest. When Beaupré died of tuberculosis in 1904 on the World's Fair Ground in St. Louis, Missouri, he was only 23. His sizeable body, displayed for profit in a store window by unscrupulous undertakers, was ordered removed by local authorities.

In 1907, Beaupré's body was discovered in a Montréal airport hangar by playing children; the circus had gone bankrupt and his cadaver was abandoned. The body of Beaupré, what is medically known as a "pathological giant," ended up mummified at the Université de Montréal where it remained for 83 years until it was cremated and returned to Willow Bunch in 1990.

The Willow Bunch Museum & Heritage Society was established in 1972 in the old hospital by a group of local students through a government summer employment program. In 1985, the museum moved to its present location in a convent school built by the Sisters of the Cross in 1914.

The "footsteps" of this Prairie giant lead to the entrance of The Willow Bunch Museum where a life-size statue and Beaupré's ashes are buried nearby. Inside, the museum houses a variety of unique and diverse artefacts such as The Willow Bunch Giant's clothing and history.

Details: *The Willow Bunch Museum and Historical Society is open May 15–Sept. 15, 10 am – 5 pm, (306) 473-2806. Off-Season: Call 24 hours in advance to arrange a visit. (306) 473-2762 or (306) 473-2279, willowbunch.ca*

If you're this far south in our province, you're probably visiting Grasslands National Park, a protected wilderness sanctuary with rolling grasslands and rugged badlands. If you like treeless, wide-open spaces, the Crossings Resort is definitely where you'll want to stay for a few days or longer — all dependent on our ever-changing Saskatchewan weather, of course.

The Crossing Resort, 30 hectares of pristine Prairie landscape, sits right on the northern boundary of Grasslands National Park (West Block), five kilometres south of the village of Val Marie, with direct access to the sprawling park.

In the 19th century, the area surrounding Val Marie was known as "The Crossing." At this spot, midway between Wood Mountain and Fort Walsh, North West Mounted Police patrols crossed the Frenchman River.

The Crossings Resort isn't a typical resort. This laid back spot doesn't feature tennis courts and swimming pools but it does rent two private vacation suites with all the creature comforts. Both suites are non-smoking and feature a kitchenette, sitting room and bedroom with half-bath attached plus a stunning view east towards 70 Mile Butte. High-speed wireless Internet is available in both suites, there's cell phone coverage and pets are welcome.

The Crossings Resort also features a campground and a solitary experience under the stars away from artificial light pollution. Since all campers don't necessarily break bread together, tent camping sites are separate from camper vans and RV spots. Eight level tent sites are accessible on a hillside and two sites can accommodate large tents for group campers. An enclosed picnic shelter with power and water are situated within the tent campground.

If you want to sleep in portable housing like Native peoples once did, seven-metre tall tipis can be rented to accommodate up to ten people each; just bring your own bedding. For the equestrian type, the Crossings offers a "Bed and Bale" service where you bring your horse to ride right into nearby Grasslands Par or rent one at lazyd.ca.

While the Crossings may seem isolated — and it is — services such as a café, grocery store, gift shop, public library and gas station can still be found five clicks north in the village of Val Marie.

Details: *The Crossing Resort is located five kilometres south of Val Marie off Highway 4 at the north end of Grasslands National Park's west gate. The resort is open year-round while the campground is open April through October only. crossingresort.com*

64   Sun Worshippers

When Pagans and Christians can unite for one June weekend in southern Saskatchewan to celebrate the sun, you just know Gravelbourg has a good vibe.

Since 2001, the Southern Saskatchewan Summer Solstice Festival (a.k.a. Summer solstice festival d'été) brings these two divergent spiritual groups together during a June weekend for a mix of culture, heritage and spirituality. This bilingual festival aims to be an inclusive cultural event that builds on the role that the Summer Solstice (June 21) has played over hundreds of years and its traditional link to agricultural cultures and communities.

Midsummer is when the sun reaches the highest point of its arc in the sky. Ancient cultures needed to mark this "solstitium" (Latin for "sun stands still") for religious and life-sustaining purposes. The lives of these agricultural cultures depended on a long growing season so without a marker of when the season had begun, they could miss days or even weeks in the growing cycle.

Many traditional solstice customs related to health and fertility for their fields. Solstice was celebrated in cities and towns with parades, pageants, plays and festivals in the market place, the town green and in the forests.

Gravelbourg, a historically francophone town of 1,400, is known as "a touch of Europe on the Prairies" with its culture, beautiful churches and other heritage architecture. The community's diverse and inexpensive solstice weekend of musical, literary and performing arts programming is for an audience of all ages, although children and seniors are a major focus.

The International Food Festival kick-starts the festival weekend on Friday evening. This component of the Solstice Fest, which highlights the cuisine of over 15 countries, is sure to attract the foodies.

Live entertainment spotlights a different nationality each year such as Polish cultural dancers or live music from Cuban, African and Middle Eastern origins. There's also a strong focus on local artists who have gained national recognition plus local up-and-comers.

Gravelbourg and area's hotels, B&Bs and three campgrounds fill up quickly on this special summer weekend, so make sure you reserve your accommodations early.

Details: *Gravelbourg is located about 110 kilometres from Moose Jaw and Swift Current and 72 kilometres south of the Trans-Canada Highway on Highway 43 and Highway 58, both paved, two-lane routes. Dates, details and event schedules: (306) 6483525, summersolsticefestivaldete.com; (306) 648-3301, gravelbourg.ca*

Early Artists at St. Victor   65

Before art galleries arrived on the scene to exhibit and sell an artist's impressions, there were petroglyphs. One of Saskatchewan's most famous spots for early human rock carvings is located near the village of St. Victor and the Big Muddy Badlands.

St. Victor Petroglyph Park is a Provincial Heritage Site located in deep, wooded coulees on the northern edge of the Wood Mountain plateau. The St. Victor Petroglyphs, over 300 carvings etched into a sandstone outcropping, depict humans and animals figures, birds, animal and human tracks (both foot and hand prints) plus several puzzling symbols.

The Plains grizzly bear is the most prevalent design, which is representative of the fact that this large mammal didn't always live far away in the Rockies. It must have been the equivalent of African lions wandering the savannah searching for food, so a Plains grizzly's diet might have included the odd human or two.

It's not known who carved these cryptic petroglyphs. Not even archaeologists can determine how old they are except that they're definitely prehistoric. Since the carvings are difficult to see, the best time of day to view and photograph is on a clear day during the morning, early evening or after a rain. After this archaeological expedition, visitors can enjoy the picnic area and watch for abundant wildlife.

During the summer, special night tours with flashlights are guided by The Friends of the Petroglyphs, an organization who manage the site. Luckily for visitors, Plains grizzly bears are no longer a concern.

Details: *Open year-round. Free admission. Located two kilometres south of St. Victor in the south-central region. Watch for signs. The Friends of the Petroglyphs, stvictor.sasktelwebsite.net or contact Monarch Lodge at St. Victor, (306) 642-5386*

66 More Bricks than Mortar

We've all heard the Prairie insult where some folks are accused of being two bricks short of a load. But not at the Claybank Brick Plant National Historic Site where there are more bricks than anything else.

The site's clever "More than Bricks and Mortar" slogan is apt for this industrial relic from the early 20th century, submerged in the hills and coulees of southern Saskatchewan. Sometimes we forget that our region has Western Canada's finest clay deposits.

This National Historic Site, virtually unchanged since it began firing bricks in 1914, is now an unlikely tourist mecca for many daytrippers from Moose Jaw and Regina or deviators off the nearby Red Coat Trail highway. Claybank offers educational brick plant tours, a café, gift shop and a hiking opportunity in the unique and adjacent badlands terrain of the Massold Clay Canyons.

Brick manufactured at Claybank adorns the facades of many prestigious buildings across Saskatchewan and Canada. "Face" brick was produced here until the 1960s and our Saskatchewan-sourced clay now adorns the majestic Gravelbourg Cathedral and many prominent public buildings such as courthouses. If you've ever stayed in the magnificent Quebec City's Chateau Frontenac, that's Claybank brick used for hotel facade improvements.

Rare "fire" brick, also produced in Claybank, lined the fire boxes of CN and CP Rail's locomotives and Corvette warships during the Second World War. This heat-resistant brick was also used for rocket launch pads at Cape Canaveral, Florida.

The plant tours, both guided and self-guided, show off Claybank's clay-based earlier economy through an educational brick-making experience called "Clay to Kiln." Visitors then file into the gift shop, located in the Bunkhouse Interpretive Centre, for Saskatchewan souvenirs that include books, postcards and local crafts. Next stop for the hungry brick-making "students" is the Bunkhouse Café with homemade meals, saskatoon berry pie and heavy, "old world" breads to haul home, baked fresh in — what else — an outdoor brick bread oven.

Details: *Claybank Brick Plant National Historic Site is located on Highway 339, only 45 minutes from Moose Jaw and one hour from Regina. Phone or check their website for guided and self-guided tours, summer hours and admission prices. (306) 868-4474, claybankbrick.ca*

West

CANADA

N

Fond-du-Lac ·   · Stony Rapids

Wollaston Lake·

La Loche·

Southend
Reindeer

Buffalo
Narrows
Œle-‡-la-Crosse · Pinehouse Lake ·   · Sandy Bay
· La Ronge   · Pelican Narrows

· Deschambault Lake

Meadow Lake·   · Montreal Lake   Cumberland
St Walburg·   House

Lloydminster·   Nipawin

Prince Albert

North   Melfort·   Tisdale   Hudson Bay
Battleford· · Rosthern
Unity·   Humboldt
Biggar · Saskatoon
Kerrobert·   · Wadena
Rosetown · Lanigan·   · Wynyard Canora
Kindersley·   · Watrous
Outlook · Davidson   Yorkton·   Kamsack
Leader· · Eston   Melville
Fort QuÕAppelle ·   Esterhazy
Gull Lake · Swift Current Moose Jaw·   Indian Head
· Regina   · Moosomin
Maple Creek ·   Griffin
Shaunavon· Gravelbourg · Assiniboia · Carlyle
· Weyburn   Carnduff
· Estevan

Scale / …chelle
75   0   75   150   225
km └──┴──┴──┴──┘ km

Fort Eco-Friendly   67

If you appreciate 19th century provincial history and want to witness 21st century environmental technology in action, Fort Battleford National Historic Site will be right up your alley.

The fort's reconstructed palisades, on a plateau above the Battle River south of the town of Battleford, commemorates the role of the North West Mounted Police at the fort from 1876 to 1885.

During the 1885 North West Rebellion, Fort Battleford was a sanctuary during the siege of Battleford. It was used as a staging base for the military operations at Cut Knife Hill, Fort Pitt, during the search for Cree Chief Big Bear and the spot where Cree Chief Poundmaker surrendered to General Middleton's forces on May 26, 1885.

Five original buildings still stand, including the officers' quarters and commanding officer's residence where Inspector Francis Dickens

(1844-86), the often-maligned third son of author Charles Dickens, was stationed. Dickens was nicknamed "Chickenstalker" by his father after the character Mrs. Chickenstalker in the Christmas book *The Chimes* that the senior Dickens was writing at the time of his son's birth. It couldn't have been much fun living in the shadow of the Victorian era's most popular author. After ploughing through his inheritance from his father, and losing an appointment in India, the hapless Francis Dickens came to Canada in 1874. His maternal aunt used her influence with family friend Lord Dufferin (then Governor General of Canada) to secure her nephew a commission in the NWMP.

Dickens first joined the NWMP as a Sub-Inspector and he remained in the force for 12 years with a promotion to Inspector in 1880. He served at Fort Walsh, Fort Macleod and Fort Pitt, from where he fled with his men to Fort Battleford during the 1885 North West Rebellion. Dickens left the force soon after and died of a heart attack a year later in Moline, Illinois.

Other than the Dickens connection, Fort Battleford is quite similar in its "military" structure to every other NWMP fort in Western Canada, even though it's a police force post, not an army base.

Fort Battleford stages an historic weapons program several times daily where one officer and three constables dressed in NWMP scarlet tunics and Strathcona leather boots fire their seven-pound cannon and small arms inside the fort. Barracks No. 5, located outside the stockade, houses a brass gatling gun and, if you want too view more antique firearms, the Fred Light Museum displays a sizeable gun collection the road back to Battleford.

Guns and green energy aren't usually linked, but since May 2006, Fort Battleford National Historic Site, unlike most of us, hasn't been inundated with monthly utility bills. The fort's visitor centre, heated and cooled with geothermal and powered by wind and solar, is Canada's first 19th century fort powered by 21st century technology.

This eco-friendly improvement, initiated in 2002 by fort manager and "Green Pioneer" Glenn Ebert, now saves on energy costs and lessens the environmental impact of the site. The centre's technology meets most of its own energy needs: when it's sunny and windy, the centre's technology produces more power than it needs and the excess power is banked as an available credit with SaskPower. When the visitor centre needs extra energy, it can draw from the SaskPower grid and that banked credit. The environment wins and the historic site wins.

Details: *Fort Battleford National Historic Site is located 153 kilometres northwest of Saskatoon off Highway 16 (the Yellowhead Route). The fort is five kilometres southeast of North Battleford on the southside of the town of Battleford. Follow the Parks Canada beaver logo signs. Open daily 9 am – 5 pm, Victoria Day weekend to Labour Day weekend. (306) 937-2621, parkscanada.ca*

68 Scotty's Dino Crib

Are you fond of hands-on museum experiences? For those adventurous spirits who crave a learning vacation, get out your pith helmet, sunscreen and work gloves. It's time to dig for dino bones.

In 1994, "Scotty" T.rex was discovered in Eastend which brought world-wide attention to this tiny town of 650 people near the Cypress Hills. Canada's most complete Tyrannosaurus rex is now on display at the T.rex Discovery Centre.

The 1,500-square-metre Centre educates its visitors with a short documentary, "The Dinosaur Hunters," which provides the backstory on Scotty's discovery and excavation. You can also spy on important work in progress by real paleontologists at the Royal Saskatchewan Museum lab, take a guided tour, or linger over the audio-visual presentations on your own timetable.

If you want to get dirty, you can sign up for a guided group tour, the Southfork Quarry Experience, where participants travel to a quarry and dig for 38-million-year-old fossils.

Curious kids can play paleontologist as they learn the difference between a plant and meat-eating dinosaur in the Discovery Dinosaurs Workshop (Grade K-3). This is where your offspring can study the anatomical differences between the dinos, create their own model and do a little digging.

The Fossil Finders dig workshop (Graded 2-12 & adult) illustrates the basics of fossil identification as you study micro fossils from the Tertiary period. This is the place to learn more about the science behind paleontology and how fossils were formed long before humans appeared in Saskatchewan.

Details: *The T.rex Discovery Centre is located just north of Eastend on the north side of the beautiful Frenchman River Valley. Open daily 9 am – 5 pm. During July and August, the Centre has extended hours, 9 am – 9 pm. Admission: Adults $8.45, Seniors $7.95, Students (over 5) $6, Children (5 and under) are free, Families $25.50. (306) 295-4009, dinocountry.com*

TAKE 5 DAVID CARPENTER
A WRITER'S FIVE WAYS TO SURVIVE
A SASKATCHEWAN WINTER

Writer David Carpenter (dccarpenter.com) is best known for his non-fiction collection of seasonal rituals, *Courting Saskatchewan*. His latest books are *Niceman Cometh* (2008), a novel set in Saskatoon, and *Welcome to Canada* (2009), a collection of stories and novellas. He's at work on a book about the history and culture of hunting in North America. David, who lives and writes in Saskatoon, is married to artist Honor Kever.

1. **Amy's on Second Restaurant, Prince Albert**. If it's winter and you're convinced that spring will never come again and you're fed up with the 4 walls of your home, the 4 corners of your tv set, computer screen, blackberry or apartment window, and if you live anywhere near Prince Albert, the remedy is easy. Just go to Amy's. This delight of a restaurant distinguishes itself from almost every other restaurant in the area: you don't eat at Amy's; you dine there. For perhaps an hour of your wintry existence you will eat food and listen to music that are both to be savoured. The only thing that I deplore about this restaurant is that, eventually, you have to leave.

2. **Spring Valley Guest Ranch, Cypress Hills**. If you're shackwacky in southwestern Saskatchewan and the winter wind is blowing constant reminders of your mortality and you feel you will never escape the ranging emptiness of this wind-devilled Prairie, fear not. South of the Trans-Canada highway, west of Eastend and south of Maple Creek is the Spring Valley Guest Ranch run by Jim Saville, the most welcoming host a Bed & Breakfast establishment has ever seen. Civil Saville, they call him. Well, actually, they don't; they call him Jim. But he has an old ranch house in a hidden valley in antelope country just a few miles from the hamlet of Ravenscrag. It is as secret and quiet and out of the way and romantic as a Zane Grey novel.

3. **Watrous and Manitou Beach**. If you're shackwacky in central Saskatchewan, so burdened by the brutality of winter that your body has decided to reject you, take your aching body to Watrous and nearby Manitou Beach, a delightfully timewarped community

that has a history of folk remedies for what ails you. Book a night or two at the spa and wallow in the waters. They are saturated with saline miracles that have never been adequately explained to me. All I know is this: the cure for your aches and pains begins, quite noticeably, in the first five minutes.

4. **Hole in the Wall, Shields Townsite**. Shackwacky in Saskatoon, for me, means leaving Saskatoon and building an igloo some-where, but that's not for everybody. Suppose you have only, say, one evening in which to regain your sanity. Jump in the car and head southeast on Highway 11 and go almost to Dundurn. Before you hit Blackstrap Lake, take a left to the community of Shields and stop at the Hole in the Wall. This is a restaurant run by a fine gent named Nelson, who is from Peru. Order everything Peruvian in sight and plan to be there for a nice long stretch. If South American Latino food is not your thing, you can order the usual stuff from the continental menu. But go there to slow down and dine with your Sig Oth and dream of places so entirely tropical that you can grow ferns in your armpits.

5. **Moose Jaw.** I think I might be saving the best for last, and I think a lot of Reginans will agree with me here. Shackwacky in southern Saskatchewan is a serious business with serious consequences for the afflicted. Winter down there is so bleak that there have been attempts to legislate against it. But wiser folk simply go to Moose Jaw, the prettiest city in all of Saskatchewan. I mean, of course, the old downtown, the part with the tunnels and the memory of Al Capone, Sin City, and best of all, the Temple Gardens Mineral Spa. Let's be honest here: there is no such thing as optimism in Saskatchewan. Even now, with a modest ongoing prosperity in evidence, even now, optimism is the province of fools. But a shackwacky person who makes the pilgrimage to Temple Gardens might discover, after gliding through the misty warmth of the pool, or after eating supper at Nits (Saskatchewan's greatest restaurant), that life is, well, entirely worth living.

Almost Canada's Little Bighorn 69

Saskatchewan's past is full of famous battles between the dominant tribe, the Cree, and their various enemies, both Native and European.

The most well-known near Cut Knife is the infamous May 2, 1885 North West Rebellion skirmish between a sizeable force under Cree Chief Poundmaker and a much smaller force under the hapless Lieutenant-Colonel William Otter of the Canadian Militia Field Force. As you can imagine, it didn't go well.

60 kilometres west of Fort Battleford is the site of the Battle of Cut Knife Hill. This is where Lieutenant-Colonel Otter and 325 men foolishly rode out from the NWMP Fort Battleford to confront an estimated 1,500 Cree, Assiniboine and Métis camped at Chief Poundmaker's Cut Knife Reserve — without Major-General Frederick Middleton's orders.

Otter was ordered by Middleton to defend Fort Battleford from attack. But why sit around cleaning your gun when there are potential medals to be won?

Eight dead and 16 wounded later, Chief Poundmaker generously allowed a reprieve to the hapless Otter and his understandably cowed troopers; they quietly stole back behind the safe palisades of Fort Battleford during the night.

It could have been Canada's Little Bighorn. If only Louis Riel had been so lucky in his dealings with Prime Minister John A. Macdonald.

Since the Battle of Cut Knife Hill marked the last time government forces were defeated during the North West Rebellion, this important — and accessible — battlefield site is worth a look.

Details: *Cut Knife Hill Battlefield Site is marked by a cairn on the same spot as the Poundmaker Interpretive Centre, six kilometres north of the town of Cut Knife on Highway 674 or 65 kilometres west of North Battleford on Highways 40 and 674.*

70 The Mounties of Fort Walsh

Viewed from the surrounding hills, the collection of buildings in the valley appears to be a daylodge at a ski resort. It's actually Fort Walsh, a North West Mounted Police post in the Cypress Hills.

Established in 1875, Fort Walsh quickly become the most important, largest and most heavily armed fort for the NWMP during the force's early years in Western Canada.

Fort Walsh was built by Inspector James Morrow Walsh and the 30 men of NWMP "B" Troop in June 1875, upstream from where the 1873 Cypress Hills Massacre occurred. The goal of Fort Walsh was to bring Canadian law and order to the area and specifically to end the local whisky trade.

Based in Fort Walsh, the garrisoned Mounties could apprehend whisky traders and horse thieves in the region plus supervise thousands of Lakota Sioux refugees, led by Chief Sitting Bull, after they fled the Battle of Little Big Horn and during the Great Sioux War of 1876-1877 in the United States. Mounties also patrolled the international border to assert Canadian sovereignty.

Fort Walsh National Historic Site of Canada has been commemorated because the fort served as headquarters of the North West Mounted Police from 1878 to 1882. This former NWMP post (circa 1878-83) was later used (1942-68) to breed horses for the force and the famous Musical Ride.

Tourists can take a guided tour of the fort's buildings, the Fort Walsh townsite, two cemeteries, a reconstructed whisky trading post, Visitor Reception Centre exhibits and, on self-guided trails, explore the ridge along Battle Creek.

Details: *Fort Walsh National Historic Site is located 55 kilometres southwest of Maple Creek, off the Trans Canada Highway. Open daily, 9:30 am – 5:30 pm from Victoria Day weekend to Labour Day weekend. After Labour Day, call the site. (306) 662-2645, parkscanada.ca/fortwalsh*

Ski Table Mountain — 71

Before there was the artificial Mount Blackstrap, there was the natural Table Mountain.

Located within Table Mountain Regional Park near North Battleford, Table Mountain Ski Area is Saskatchewan's oldest and best sliding hill. Table's valley slopes offer some of the best skiing and snowboarding in Saskatchewan without enduring a midwinter ten-hour drive.

In 1969, Battlefords Ski Club members, who had been operating from nearby Prongua Hill, decided to find a larger hill to operate a ski facility. These people were serious about their sliding and apparently not afraid to work to make it happen. During the summer and fall of 1969, 135 hectares of land were leased but they still needed a day lodge. The club bought the town of Battleford's railway station, moved it onto the land, installed electric power, purchased equipment, built a rope tow and cleared ski runs.

Table Mountain opened for the 1970–1971 ski season while Mount Blackstrap workers had just finished piling the last of 900,000 cubic metres of soil and rock near Dundurn a few months earlier. The ski club's efforts didn't go unnoticed. The provincial government created Table Mountain Regional Park and the official opening on December 5, 1973 meant free night skiing for all who owned the cumbersome boots and skis of the time.

Battleford's former train station/Table's day lodge was replaced in 1989 by a 1,000-square-metre chalet along with a new parking lot to accommodate the next generation of sliders. During the summer of 1991, Table Mountain's 600-metre quad chairlift was installed. Table Mountain's 25th anniversary celebrations in January 1995 saw Nancy Greene races and the original "Crazy Canuck," "Jungle Jim" Hunter, in attendance.

By 1996, the knuckle-draggers (including me) were officially welcomed when a snowboard terrain park was constructed that summer. During the winter of 1998–99, even the truck tube enthusiasts were embraced with a brand new tubing park.

The big recent improvement, which takes this "regional resort" to the next level for its users, was the 2004 complete renovation of the day lodge that includes a licensed lounge, a full-meals cafeteria, satellite television and a handcrafted flagstone fireplace.

Sure, you can spend a whack of money to go to the mountains for expensive high-speed quads while dealing with queue-jumping European tourists — or you can stick to the accessible, affordable and 100 percent man-made snow covered runs of Table Mountain.

Details: *Lifts run 10 am – 4:30 pm, December to March (weather permitting). Friday night skiing is cancelled if the mercury dips below –20. Table Mountain is located 16 kilometres west of Battleford or 29 kilometres east of Cut Knife on Highway 40 then 9.5 kilometres north and west on a grid road. (306) 937-2920, tablemountainregionalpark.com*

TAKE 5 GREG HUSZAR
A PHOTOGRAPHER'S FIVE
LOCATIONS FOR SHUTTERBUGS

Greg Huszar (greghuszarphotography.com) is one of Saskatchewan's leading commercial photographers. Because Greg's commercial photography business is 90 percent location work, and since his photography for national clients takes him from coast to coast, it means he spends significant chunks of time on the road. Yet Greg wouldn't live anywhere else. He loves Saskatchewan's varied but minimalist landscape: beautiful lakes and forests up north plus great attractions in the south. Although Greg has exhibited his work in Toronto, the majority of his work is seen on billboards, brochures and websites around the country. Greg's biggest photography tip: leave the Trans-Canada Highway! Quirky Saskatchewan offers abandoned buildings, gas stations and rusty cars in a sea of Prairie grass and it's everywhere; carry your camera and stop often.

1. **Cypress Hills Interprovincial Park.** The whole park is amazing. The glaciers passed by the region so the Cypress Hills stick up out of the Prairie. There are forests of lodgepole pines with deep valleys and ponds full of wildlife, many great lookouts with 80-kilometre views and historic Fort Walsh; it offers great opportunities for people who love to shoot still-lifes and you'll find fort staff dressed in period clothing.

2. **Missinipe on the Churchill River.** This hamlet on Otter Lake, fed by the Churchill River, and 80 clicks north of La Ronge, is in the Canadian Shield so the whole area consists of rock, moss and forest. Since there are plenty of people canoeing and kayaking, the river and forests are excellent places to shoot outdoor adventure sports plus Otter Lake is a floatplane launch. From Missinipe, you can access the beautiful Nistowiak Falls by boat or plane and the eco-region is home to the second largest bald eagle nesting grounds in North America.

3. **La Reata Ranch near Kyle**. Situated on the beautiful shores of Diefenbaker Lake, Le Reata Ranch provides many opportunities for landscapes of the lake and its rolling hills. Talk to the owner, George, and photograph daily life on a working ranch where city slickers go to learn how to become cowboys.

4. **The Great Sand Hills**. This is our very own miniature desert on the Prairies. You can shoot this unique, beautiful landscape that looks like you're actually in the Sahara.

5. **Castle Butte in the Big Muddy Badlands.** This is where you'll find great vistas, unusual landscape — and the possibility of snakes.

In 1968, Winnipeg entrepreneur Ray Olecko developed the Boler trailer, a modest little home-away-from-home. It was the world's first fibreglass-moulded travel-trailer, shaped like a squared egg.

These affordable, utilitarian trailers, priced at $1,400, were a big hit with Canadian families because two adults and two children could comfortably camp in them without suffering the downside of a tent-trailer: rainy day leaks.

Olecko's invention now enjoys cult status among Boler collectors. Drive down any back lane in Saskatchewan and you're certain to spot Canada's budget Airstream trailer parked beside the garage or left in the backyard to be used for extra houseguests.

Olecko was selling cars when he became fascinated with the potential of fibreglass. His first invention was a fibreglass septic tank and his design, two halves bolted together, was lightweight and easy to ship in comparison with the steel and concrete tanks of the day. His patented design quickly became an industry standard. While camping with his family in a tent-trailer, Olecko began to envision a lightweight fibreglass trailer.

Some call the Boler "The Septic Tank on Wheels." Not all needs were met, though. Although based on his original septic tank design, Olecko's 13-foot pods do not feature a toilet or shower. Ray Olecko is now deceased, but his Boler vision endures. Hundreds of Boler enthusiasts assemble each summer in campgrounds across Canada to swap stories, admiration and parts. Earlton, Ontario, where a Boler franchise factory was located in the 1970s, beat Saskatchewan to it in 2001 with the first-ever Boler gathering.

Not to be outdone, organizers Greg Pittman and Lisa Vanderwiel of Saskatoon held the first Saskatchewan "Bolerama" in 2002 at Saskatchewan Landing Provincial Park, which drew 18 Bolers and their keener owners.

This community-in-a-campground have since met in the Cypress Hills, at White City outside Regina and in the past few years, at Macklin Lake Regional Park for four days during the third week of July. Bolerama — now known as the "Prairie Egg Gathering" — attracts close to 100 Boler enthusiasts who arrive from the Prairie provinces, other parts of Canada and even the United States.

Details: *Got a Boler trailer to show off? Then join this community of Boler enthusiasts for their next Prairie Egg Gathering. Visit geocities.com/bolerama for more info.*

Desert Sand Between Your Toes 73

Lawrence of Arabia would have felt right at home in the Great Sandhills — at least for those too few hot months of the year anyway.

The southern section of our province is now mostly cultivated Prairie. But a small — yet accessible — desert topography amongst the farmland is an anomaly to be celebrated, explored and protected.

Located south of the South Saskatchewan River near Leader, the Great Sandhills, spread out over 1,900 square kilometres, is worth a closer look.

This mix of sand dunes, grasslands, hills, saline lakes, pebble plains, cotton wood groves and aspen bluffs have been settled or ranched over a hundred years yet the majority of land remains in provincial ownership.

Many dunes rise to 15 metres and cover several hectares, second only in Canada to the Athabasca Sand Dunes in our northern boreal forest. During sunset, the golden light turns the dunes red and highlights the surface ripples. The Sandhills are affected by mighty northwest winds and have been clocked moving eastwards at a rate of four metres annually.

The Great Sandhills are the largest remaining contiguous native Prairie area in the province. Home to a wide spectrum of native plants and animals, including species at risk, the dunes are fringed by small clumps of trees that include aspen, birch, willow, and by rose bushes, sagebrush and chokecherry.

Saskatchewan once contained an estimated 24 million hectares of intact Prairie ecosystems. Now, less than one million are considered to be in good ecological condition (roughly four percent) that includes our sandy nugget near the Alberta boundary.

Many visitors take the "Leader Loop," a self-directed, regional tour that begins in the town of Leader. The first stop is to the old CNR Caboose where you'll find maps, brochures and souvenirs then the tour continues on to the village of Sceptre and eventually into the Great Sandhills.

While in Sceptre, check out the Great Sandhills Museum where you can "take a walk through the pages of time" down the museum's wooden boardwalks and experience visits — via the diorama-esque theme rooms — to a boarding house, hospital, livery stable, school, church, interpretive centre and dentist office.

Details: *Leader Tourism is open Victoria Day weekend to Labour Day, 10 am – 6 pm and on shorter hours September to May, (306) 628-3995, leader.ca/landscapes; Great Sandhills Museum, Sceptre, (306) 623-4345, greatsandhillsmuseum.com*

Many of our pioneer parents, grandparents and great-grandparents would have stories of early life in a sod house. And most of them probably wish they never had to set eyes on one again.

Prior to 1914, sod houses were an integral part of the Prairie landscape during the Western Canadian settlement period. My maternal grandmother, Mary Eleanor Simpson, was born in her homesteader parent's sod house, very close to the oldest, continuously occupied sod building in Saskatchewan.

Since 1910, the Addison family has lived in this oddity from Saskatchewan's pioneer period. During the first important months and years of establishing their farm, most homesteaders constructed a "soddy" as a temporary shelter. Since there was very little lumber or even brick available for early homesteaders in treeless areas of the province, most built their homes of sod, which is a slab of Prairie grass with an attached clump of topsoil.

A sod house was an uncomfortable home that rapidly crumbled and when the homesteader could afford the building materials, it was replaced with a stick-frame house.

In 1909, English immigrant James Addison set out by ox cart from Saskatoon in 1909 to his new homestead northeast of Kindersley. He immediately noticed that most sod homes in the region deteriorated in a few months or years. This scrappy pioneer was determined to build a home that would stand up against our harsh climate for his wife Jane and their two children, so he started work on what would become an architecturally unique home.

When it was completed in 1911, the structure's sloped walls were well over a metre thick and protected by a truss system wood roof. Addison even built a similarly designed barn that unfortunately sat in the path of a twister one summer.

James and Jane Addison's solid soddy still stands and modern improvements include indoor plumbing and electricity in the 1960s. The property also features a farmyard that includes a mature garden, barn, two sheds, a dugout and a shelterbelt.

Addison's third child, Edith, who was only a year old when the Addison Sod House was constructed, still lives in the Addison Sod House, now a Provincial Heritage Property.

Details: *The Addison Sod House National Historic Site is located 16 kilometres north of Kindersley on Highway 21 then 10 kilometres east on a grid road. Call ahead. (306) 463-3364, tpcs.gov.sk.ca/PHP-booklet-addison-sod-house*

Home of the Startini   75

If I ever decide to open a great café and grill in a Saskatchewan town with an actual sense of architectural heritage, I'd do it like the Star Café & Grill.

Located off the Trans-Canada highway in the town of Maple Creek, the Star Café & Grill brings a metropolitan dining atmosphere to a restored *fin-de-siecle* stone structure — all in a rolling landscape right out of a Wallace Stegner tale of the Old West.

When the tired old building you live and paint in comes up for sale, what would you do? Barry Weiss, who lived upstairs above this former Chinese café, decided to take the plunge with two other partners, buy the building then open south-western Saskatchewan's funkiest heritage restaurant, which features the best intimate dining experience between Regina and Calgary.

The Star's menu is tailored to the seasons and the chefs make the extra effort to provide fresh and varied flavours, sourced both locally and globally. Located in the heart of cattle country, the Star Cafe & Grill serves local beef to people who know what great beef is all about. At lunch, premium beer on tap is served up with handmade sirloin burgers, filet mignon paninis, and shaved prime rib sandwiches that accompany home-made soups, fresh salads and pastas.

Diners start off their evening culinary experience with inspired "Startinis" and a carefully selected wine list. Appetisers include mussels, coconut prawns and scallops then it's on to steaks, prime rib and ribs with the Star's own Jack Daniel barbecue sauce. These entrées

and lighter meals like the chicken supreme or a delicate salmon satisfy both locals and regional visitors. Decadent desserts like the famous chocolate caramel chimichanga conclude a gourmet meal in Maple Creek's new landmark.

The rare and shrouded building, built in the 1890s from field stones collected south of Maple Creek, was hanging by a thread at the time and a new owner could just as easily have bulldozed it into history. All three partners, Weiss, Dave Turner and Tina Cresswell were committed to the preservation of one of Maple Creek's historical properties so they threw caution to the wind and created a beautiful restaurant in a town of only 2,900 inhabitants.

The original Star was an old-style Chinese café that had bounced around various locations in Maple Creek since the 1940s. The three partners breathed new life into the old name but changed the cuisine, decor and engaged in extensive structural repairs to the building.

The interior concept is to reflect and honour the mercantile past of the space. The restored tongue-and-groove walls and ceiling are original and the new floor was salvaged hemlock from the roof of a Second World War hangar in Fort Macleod, Alberta. The reproduction bar is the partners' own nod to a classic long bar — now long gone — from the bar in Maple Creek's landmark Commercial Hotel, a few doors down.

Details: *Open for lunch Tues. to Fri. 11–2, and for dinner Tues. to Sun., 5–8:30 (reservations recommended). 32 Pacific Avenue, Maple Creek, (306) 662-2202, thestarcafe.ca*

76   The Allan Sapp Gallery

If you want to appreciate life on a Native reserve in 1930s Saskatchewan, look no farther than this significant gallery dedicated to the life's work of painter Allen Sapp.

Sapp, a Plains Cree born in 1928 on the Red Pheasant Reserve in west-central Saskatchewan, is Saskatchewan's most celebrated artist. Yet, as a child, he could neither read nor write; instead, he found refuge and satisfaction in drawing pictures.

A sickly child, Sapp was raised by his grandmother. On his sick bed one dramatic night, she gave him the Cree name Kiskayetum ("he perceives it"). Luckily for him and for us, Sapp survived his childhood illness and continued to draw and paint.

As an adult, Sapp moved from the reserve to North Battleford with his wife and young family where he sold his art on the street to support them. One fateful day, he was on his sales rounds at a local medical clinic when he made a new friend and future patron, Dr. Allan Gonor. (It's Gonor's collection of Sapp's realist depiction of reserve life that now makes up the bulk of the Allen Sapp Gallery.)

After Gonor began to collect his work, interest grew in Sapp's paintings. In 1969, Sapp's solo show at the Mendel Art Gallery in Saskatoon turned out to be an enormous career boost; soon after he became a critical and international success.

The self-taught artist has since been awarded a membership with the prestigious Royal Canadian Academy of Artists, a Saskatchewan Award of Merit and an Order of Canada.

Next time you're on your way through North Battleford, stop in to view this celebrated Saskatchewan artist's dynamic work.

Details: *The Allen Sapp Gallery is located at #1 Railway Ave. E. in North Battleford. Open Summer: 11 am – 5 pm; September: Wed.–Sun., 12–4 pm; and Winter (October–Victoria Day), Wed.–Sun., 1–5 pm, (306) 445-1760, allensapp.com*

Singletrack in the Cypress Hills | 77

We may not have mountains, but many of us own mountain bikes. So where do we go to burn off the winter fat and explore nature without creating deep lug-tire ruts?

Singletrack enthusiasts can chose from over 20 established trail systems around the province. However, southwest Saskatchewan's easily accessible terrain encompasses ravines and valleys that offer up challenging mountain biking trails for all rider levels.

At 1,466 metres above sea level, Cypress Hills Interprovincial Park is higher than the summit of B.C.'s Rogers Pass on the Trans-Canada Highway. This highest point of land in southern Canada between the Rockies and Labrador offers the finest views of the surrounding plains and that gigantic summer sun sliding behind the horizon.

The Saskatchewan side of the Cypress Hills Interprovincial Park serves up novice to expert mountain bike trails. Along a plateau that stretches for over 120 kilometres above the surrounding Prairie, riders can experience multi-use hike/bike/ski trails and brilliant single-track sections through forest, beside streams and around lakes.

Hardcore riders will especially want to check out the West Block where, on certain trails, banging your tires over protruding tree roots feels just like riding through a mountain watershed. This anomalous alpine region mixes Prairie grasslands alongside lodge pole pine forest, rocky outcroppings and other mountain characteristics. Botany-minded riders should be able to spot over 18 species of rare orchids plus elk, deer, moose, fox, lynx, bobcat and over 200 bird species.

Details: *Cypress Hills Interprovincial Park is located 27 kilometres south of Maple Creek on Highway 21. (306) 662-5411, tpcs.gov.sk.ca/CypressHills. Ask park attendants for maps and information on how to access the bike trails or purchase the inexpensive Saskatchewan Mountain Bike Manual and Trail Guide through the Saskatchewan Cycling Association, saskcycling.ca*

78 A Hobby Gone Bad in the Cypress Hills

Forget about B.C.'s Okanagan or Ontario's Niagara region for your next wine tour. Those popular destinations only grow grapes. Saskatchewan's Cypress Hills Vineyard & Winery may grow and produce two quality grape wines but they're mostly known on the Prairies for their six fruit wines. But this isn't the same stuff Prairie teens nipped at from a recycled rye bottle, slyly culled from our grandparents' basement "wine cellar."

Canada's newest wine destination — and Saskatchewan's first commercial vineyard and winery — is tucked into the edge of Cypress Hills Interprovincial Park, the highest point of land in southern Canada between the Rockies and Labrador. According to Marty and Marie Bohnet, when asked about why they'd build a winery in the middle of nowhere, their short answer is: "It's a hobby gone bad!"

This 2007 Saskatchewan Tourism "Rookie of the Year" Award Winner offers self-guided tours of the vineyards and guided tours of the winemaking area where curious visitors can learn about enology on-the-ground. While surrounded by the stunning high country scenery, a filling lunch is served on The Winery Bistro's patio that includes artisan cheese platters and home-made saskatoon pie.

Then it's time to taste their eight offered wines. Sure, they'll put out their own cabernet for a tasting during a Saskatchewan version of the movie, *Sideways*. Ask the Bohnets to pull out the hard stuff: the fruit wines.

Sample, then tuck away a bottle of saskatoon chokecherry, sour cherry, rhubarb blend, black currant & honey wine or a mead dessert wine made with local honey that will make your next dinner guests ask you about those bold tones and where they can get a bottle or two for themselves.

Marty Bohnet's family has ranched in the Cypress Hills for generations with no real history of wine making on either side of their families. Like so many people, the Bohnets started making wine in

1994 under the encouragement — or "bad influence" as they put it — of some friends. In 1995, they plunked in their first three grape wines that actually flourished in southwest Saskatchewan's hot, arid climate. By the third year they had enough grapes to make a small batch of wine.

In 2003, the BSE crisis hit hard with Prairie ranching families. It was Marty Bohnet's idea to diversify into a vineyard operation. In spring 2004, the Bohnets set out on their wine adventure, were licensed to make wine in 2005, built the winery in 2006 and opened it to the public in June 2007. Now there's a vineyard gift shop with an array of uniquely Saskatchewan and wine-associated items, including their eight Saskatchewan-produced wines.

Why travel all the way to the Okanagan when it's all here in Saskatchewan's new wine region?

Details: *Open May 15–Dec. 20. Located 20 kilometres southwest of Maple Creek on the paved Hwy 271 near Fort Walsh National Historic Site and Cypress Hills Interprovincial Park (28 kilometres off the Trans-Canada Highway). Services include a large turnaround area for motor coaches and travel-trailers, a wheelchair accessible building, patio and bathrooms. Well-behaved pets and children welcome. Bus tours are also available. (306) 662-4100, cypresshillswinery.com*

Sagebrush Sanctuary 79

Some people can't wait to hive off and create art, often in an isolated location.

In 1996, artists Dean and Fran Francis embarked on an ambitious project just 50 kilometres south of Dean's original family farm. Dean

Francis says they just wanted to be out there, to have a studio and to create art in their home and work space, located west of Leader right by the Alberta boundary.

When his hometown church in Mantario came up for sale, Dean bought it and moved it south onto their 32-hectare acreage. It's now one of three churches on the property devoted to art-making and exhibition.

They've now filled the space around their re-purposed buildings with eight hectares of landscaping and scenic gardens that include Russian olive shrubs, spruce and pine, skunk bush, native flower beds, lilacs, saskatoon bushes, chokecherries and snowberries. The arid climate has made them focus on trees and hardy shrub and the abundance of berry bushes is a particular songbird enticement.

Since gardening and renovation occupy their summers, both artists find that the quiet Saskatchewan winters provide the perfect pause for them to get into the studio. A landscape painter, Dean has depicted the local area on canvas for 30 years, while Fran, who also paints and draws, has focused on pottery for 15 years.

When the gallery space finally opened to the public in 2001, Dean and Fran were able to work on their art for a full year and then bring it out in the spring to sell. They'd like to take a break from all the renovating and gardening so Dean can paint and Fran can throw clay year-round, but they say they just can't stop "scheming" and that just like in art, there's always room for improvement.

Details: *Sagebrush Studios is located 20 kilometres east of Empress, Alta. on the Saskatchewan side of the provincial boundary. It's open to visitors from the Victoria Day weekend to Labour Day and by appointment the rest of the year. 1-877-565-2039, deanfrancis.ca*

80 Old Man on His Back

As industrial agriculture continues to dominate the Prairie land-scape, a part of Canada's Big Empty has been lost. Saskatchewan's grasslands are rapidly disappearing as cultivated crops overtake the semi-arid, mixed grass Prairie that was once one of North America's major ecosystems.

Thanks to the generosity of Peter and Sharon Butala, who donated 5,300 hectares of their own ranchland then stocked it with 50 Plains bison, these grasslands in the southwest are being restored to their former unkempt glory. The Butalas dubbed the preserve "Old Man on His Back Prairie and Heritage Conservation Area" (OMB).

Author Sharon Butala moved to the area in 1976 when she mar-

ried cowboy-rancher Peter Butala. The dramatic landscape quickly became her chief source of angst and inspiration: "I found it all moving and terrible, at its best and worst reaching through the layers of cultural artifice — televisionland, country and western culture, agribusiness, and Euro-Canadian ancestor worship — to the depths of the human condition. I did not love it, often I hated it, but even then I could not wrench my eyes and my heart away. Nor my pen," writes Butala on her website.

Literary tourists can enrich their visit to OMB by first reading Sharon Butala's *Coyote's Morning Cry, The Perfection of Morning* and *Wild Stone Heart.* Or you can just take in the landscape, the wildlife and experience it directly: savour the wide-open vistas of the Prairies, the endless technicolour sunsets, the riotous display of native wildflowers and the long-billed curlew and ferruginous hawk.

Among the other wildlife on the property are small herds of pronghorn antelope, the endangered burrowing owl and the swift fox which, once numerous, are slowly making a comeback.

At the new Visitor's Centre, you can learn more about the history of the land and the delicate relationship between ranching and the environment. Because of ranchland donated by the Butalas, the OMB grasslands has been preserved in perpetuity by the Nature Conservancy of Canada so visitors can enjoy this beautiful example of native Prairie for many years to come.

Details: *The Visitors Centre, which portrays the history of the land and the delicate relationship between ranching and the environment, is open on weekends from May to September. Visitors should contact the T.rex Discovery Centre in Eastend for current travel information. (306) 295-4009, dinocountry.com*

East

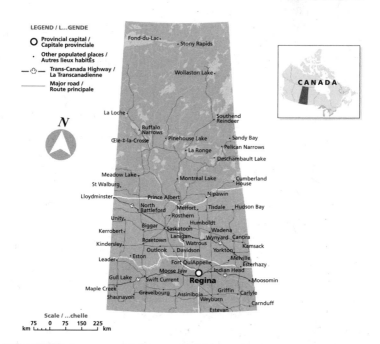

Provincial capital /
Capitale provinciale

Other populated places /
Autres lieux habitÉs

Trans-Canada Highway /
La Transcanadienne

Major road /
Route principale

CANADA

N

Scale / ...chelle
75   0   75   150   225
km   km

---

81   Captain Pierce's Pups

In the late 19th century, if you failed in Europe, Western Canada was definitely the place to reinvent yourself.

That's what Captain Edward Mitchell Pierce did. This failed English gentleman came to Canada to start again in a new land full of promise. Or so he hoped. Captain Pierce established Cannington Manor in 1882, southeast of what is now Moose Mountain Provincial Park.

Pierce didn't just step off a westbound train with big new ideas. No, he brought along a wife and eight children from Old Blighty. First he built a log farmhouse to accommodate his sizeable family.

Then, keenly aware that the country he left behind teemed with idle rich young men whose perturbed parents couldn't wait to kick them loose, Pierce decided to establish a Victorian English agricultural colony with an agricultural college. This entrepreneurial scheme was an effort by Pierce to teach young bachelors from England's privileged classes — who had failed to live up to the strict aristocratic expectations of the time — to farm instead.

These "Remittance Men," who received a scheduled remittance or allowance from their families, were often second sons. Under British tradition, these individuals didn't expect to inherit anything from their family's estate. Payments were made to keep the young man away from Britain where it was thought he would cause problems for his family. For a better picture of the period, think Prince Harry, a regular remittance payment and a waterfall of gin getting in the way of responsibility and gainful employment.

Pierce's ex-urbanite pupils, known as "pups," were charged £100 a year, which included farming lessons, room-and-board and all the boredom you could stuff into an 1880s Prairies farm day.

Shockingly, most of the wealthy English lads were not interested agriculturalists. Instead, they emulated the lives they'd left behind as gentlemen of leisure. Instead of ploughing, seeding and sweating in the midday sun like mad dogs, these Englishmen's days were filled with tennis, cricket, football, billiards, thoroughbred racing, polo matches, theatrical plays, fox hunting and numerous social events.

Although the death of Captain Pierce in 1888 might have meant the end of Cannington Manor, by the mid-1890s, over 200 people resided in this little slice of England which continued on with an Anglo cultural and recreational life. However, by 1900, maintaining Victorian England social customs on the Canadian Prairies proved to be too much and the village of Cannington Manor was eventually abandoned.

Original and reconstructed buildings still stand at Cannington Manor Provincial Historic Park. Exhibits and interpreters in period costume help re-create the heyday of this odd — but short — Little England on the Prairies.

Details: *Cannington Manor is located 16 kilometres southeast of Moose Mountain Provincial Park, west and north of Highway 603. Open 10 am – 5 pm daily (except Tues.), Victoria Day weekend to Labour Day. Limited facilities include a picnic area, washrooms and drinking water, but no gin. $9/family, $4/adult, $1/student. (306) 577-2600, tpcs.gov.sk.ca/CanningtonManor*

82   Yorkton's Short Flicks

Sure, Toronto has their film festival every September, but every May, Yorkton has the distinction of hosting the longest running film festival of its kind in North America.

Over the years, the Yorkton Short Film & Video Festival has garnered an esteemed reputation as one of Canada's top short film and video festivals. In a period of pirated downloads and often mediocre YouTube videos, Yorkton's cinefest has a reputation that attracts outstanding entries and personalities from across Canada.

Established in 1947 as the Yorkton Film Council, Canada's first short film & video festival started one October evening in 1950. The projector whirred and the first film of the first Yorkton International Documentary Film Festival filled the screen at Yorkton City Hall.

The festival was the brainchild of James Lysyshyn. Lysyshyn, a young National Film Board field officer, had been stationed in Saskatchewan with a mandate to set up film councils in his area of jurisdiction, which eventually included Yorkton. Since arts festival were often held in Europe and music and science festivals could be found in other parts of Canada at the time, Lysyshyn came up with the idea for a film festival. At the time Yorkton had a very active film council organized by Dave Sharples, who had been a wartime projectionist. Lysyshyn decided to pitch his idea to them.

Entries for the first festival in 1950 came from India, Brazil, Denmark, Australia, Switzerland, Sweden, the United States and Britain. Canada had many entries, including five from Saskatchewan. At the first festival, the audience selected the National Film Board's *The Royal Winter Fair* as the winning film. Second and third place went to entries from India and the United States.

The first Golden Sheaf Award, introduced in 1958, has been presented to the most outstanding film entry in the festival ever since. Held in the Gallagher Centre, the Golden Sheaf Awards are presented in 21 genre categories and three craft awards categories.

Some very interesting Canadians have visited the festival, including Bruno Gerussi, Gordon Pinsent and Barry Morse. Film awards have been won by Cordell Barker, twice nominated for Oscars, and Frederic Bach, who went on to win two Oscars for his work.

The Yorkton Short Film & Video Festival has undergone many changes since its inception. In 2009, the festival established the Ruth Shaw Award for Best Saskatchewan Production. (Ruth Shaw, the last of the original festival members, is now over 90.)

From the kick-off party to screenings to the Gala, the Yorkton Film Festival is jam-packed with exciting events, including a number of workshops where attendees can rub elbows with industry experts.

Details: *The Yorkton Short Film & Video Festival runs for four days every May. (306) 782-7077, goldensheafawards.com*

83 Avian Mecca

Saskatchewan is home to a wide variety of shorebirds and a number of saline sanctuaries for our fowl friends. If you're an avian fancier or would like to be, then I have a place for you.

If you usually only stop your highway-bound vehicle for gas, this may be the perfect season for the family to take up birding — a great form of slow tourism.

Stretch those weary legs on the long haul along Highway 16 (the Yellowhead) between Saskatoon and Yorkton at the Quill Lakes International Bird Area (QLIBA). Since one million birds visit the region annually, three towns — Wynyard, Foam Lake and Wadena — cooperate to host east-central Saskatchewan's bird watching project in this premiere birding locale.

QLIBA's gateway area just off the Yellowhead is the best access to the Foam Lake Heritage Marsh. The marsh, managed by Ducks

TAKE 5 GENE MAKOWSKY
A ROUGHRIDER'S FIVE SIDELINE ESCAPES

Offensive lineman Gene Makowsky (#60) was born and raised in Saskatoon where he played four seasons with the University of Saskatchewan Huskies. Drafted in the second round (23rd overall) of the 1995 CFL College Draft, he's played all of his 15+ CFL seasons with the Roughriders. Gene has been named the CFL's Most Outstanding Lineman in 2004 and 2005 and he was named a CFL all-star for the fourth consecutive season in 2007, the same year that he helped to win a Grey Cup for the Riders — their first since 1989. When he's not playing against the Riders' sworn enemies or spending time with his family — Tammy and their three sons — Gene is a substitute teacher in Regina where he also contributes time to a number of charitable activities.

1. **Mosaic Stadium**. I'm probably a little biased here, but the next best thing to playing for the Roughriders is attending a home game at the old stadium. To blend in, make sure to wear green face paint or a watermelon helmet and cheer very loudly for the home team. The atmosphere on a warm summer's evening is something every Saskatchewanian should experience at least once. There's no place I'd rather be.

2. **Deer Valley Golf.** There are so many excellent golf courses in Saskatchewan, it's difficult to choose a favourite. But Deer Valley is quickly becoming the choice for my teammates and I. This relatively new course is 20 minutes northwest of Regina and it's worth the drive. It features a very picturesque and challenging layout, probably too hard for this hacker, but the vistas are worth checking out

Unlimited Canada, spans 1,600 hectares of wetland wonders. It's the perfect habitat for nesting waterfowl and therefore a perfect venue for alert viewers to enjoy sightings of shorebirds, waterfowl and songbirds.

There are self-guided tours, lookouts and hiking trails. The best part of this marshy habitat is that just like the birds, humans get to visit for free. Pack a lunch, your comfortable hiking shoes, and enjoy the Yellowhead's secret bird sanctuary.

For those of you who aren't in a hurry to get on your way, you can head north of the Yellowhead on Highway 35 to the town of Wadena for more birding. Wadena's wetlands are a quick five-

even if you don't golf. Deer Valley is always in good shape and, like most golf in the province, the value is better than anywhere else.

3. **Wascana Park**. The grounds that surround the awesome Legislative Building in Regina are really impressive. The first time I went there was when I began to play for the Riders. I couldn't believe I was in Regina: a large lake surrounded by trees, playgrounds, picnic sites, sports fields and walking paths that branch out in all directions are all part of this urban oasis.

4. **Batoche National Historic Site**. Most people assume you have to go to Europe or at least Central Canada to experience history. The most interesting part of Canadian history to me happened right here in Saskatchewan with the 1885 North West Rebellion. You can decide this for yourself an hour northeast of Saskatoon. You'll see where Métis fighters were dug-in during Canada's first naval battle on the South Saskatchewan River and the bullet holes on the town rectory. The fact that I can still remember my Grade 12 trip to Batoche quite clearly speaks to how fascinating this place really is.

5. **Good Spirit Lake.** After a long cold winter, it's always nice spending some time by a lake during the summer. There are so many great locations in Saskatchewan to sit on the beach, enjoy water sports or fish. I like Good Spirit because of great memories I had there as a kid (it was close to the family farm near Canora) plus the great resort and golfing experiences available to visitors.

minute drive outside of town on the shores of the scenic Little Quill Lake. For an extended visit, meander along the five trails ("Wildflower Way" features a wildflower-strewn pathway) and view pelicans, black-crowned night herons and marbled godwits.

If you're feeling spry, you might want to take your canoe off the roof at their canoe launch and get right into the lake among the birds. For landlubbers, there are picnic and washroom facilities, boardwalks and two observation towers, so don't forget to pack your binoculars. You may even need more than one set if the kids are along for the trip.

Since it's part of the prestigious Western Hemispheric Shorebird Reserve, you won't want to miss this watery venue.

Details: *The Quill Lakes International Bird Area is open year-round. Birders can visit the QLIBA website or contact the communities affiliated with all three birding sites: Wadena, (306) 338-2145; Foam Lake, (306) 272-3359; and Wynyard, (306) 554-2123, quill-lakes-bird-area.com*

84 A Mountain Called Duck

Nobody else in Canada would name a mountain after a duck except maybe Manitoba who share our eastern "mountain." But since surveyor John Palliser found it full of ducks in 1865, then so be it.

The Duck Mountain Highlands, a picturesque part of east-central Saskatchewan on the Manitoba boundary, is rife with rolling hills and clean lakes in a boreal forest setting.

While Duck Mountain Provincial Park may ape northern Saskatchewan in its topography, this green gem bordering the grain belt is merely a southerly piece of boreal uplands. That's a good thing for those of us who want a quiet park escape within roughly three hours of both Regina and Saskatoon — and even closer if you live in Yorkton, Canora or Kamsack.

Duck Mountain, a 26,160-hectare, four-season park, features accommodations that range from seven campgrounds and 466 sites to Duck Mountain Lodge's modern cabins and townhouses. It also offers full days of recreational opportunities.

The spring-fed Madge Lake is stocked with pike, walleye and perch while Jackfish Lake is the place to cast for rainbow and tiger trout; the park even rents boats. Horseback riding, miniature golf and its grown-up sibling, an 18-hole course, compete for leisure time with hiking or biking a section of the Trans-Canada Trail.

If you're visiting during the winter, this hilly park offers 50 kilometres of groomed cross-country ski trails (and another 20 kilometres of backcountry), equipment rentals in the Duck Mountain Lodge (call ahead) plus a day lodge, waxing room, snack bar and six warming shelters. Trail maps are available on the park's website.

For the competitive skier, the Kamsack Cross Country Ski Club partners with the park in late February to host the annual Duck Mountain Cross Country Ski Loppet.

Details: *Duck Mountain Provincial Park is 23 kilometres northeast of Kamsack on Highway 57. Duck Mountain is a Reserve-a-Site park (saskparks.net); (306) 542-5513, tpcs.gov.sk.ca/DuckMountain; Duck Mountain Lodge, (306) 542-3466, madgelake.ca*

85 Danceland at Manitou Beach

Dancing has always been popular at Manitou Beach. In the 1920s, three dance halls offered places to kick up your heels every day of the week, including a Sunday "midnight frolic."

Moose Jaw entrepreneur Wellington White built Danceland pavilion in 1928 beside Little Manitou Lake to accompany his indoor soaking pool. The "Dead Sea of the Prairies" is chock full of healing magnesium and sulphate and in the 1920s, this lake community was once the most popular summer resort on the Prairies; it even rivalled Banff's Hot Springs.

Danceland boasts a maple dance floor that hides a thick layer of horsehair bought from local farmers and imported from Quebec. When popular Jitney (nickel) dances were staged in the early days, they caused Danceland's nail-less floor to bounce like a trampoline to Mart Kenny & his Western Gentlemen and Don Messer & his Islanders.

It's still open year-round and if you attend the Square & Pattern Dancing Weekends, watch your head on the ceiling. That floor still bucks like a wild bronco.

Details: *For scheduled dances and events, call 1-800-267-5037 or danceland.ca*

86 Soak and Float

About two hours north of Moose Jaw's Temple Gardens Mineral Spa, you'll find Saskatchewan's second soaking spot in the lakeside village of Manitou Beach.

For hundreds of years, the water of Little Manitou Lake, fed by underground springs, has been credited with the relief of aches,

pains and skin ailments. That's because this shallow, saline lake has a specific gravity 10 percent higher than regular water because of a higher concentration of dissolved salts and minerals.

Known as the "lake of the healing waters," Native medicine men named it "Manitou" since they believed the Great Spirit bestowed it upon their people.

Next to the lake you'll find the budget-minded Manitou Springs Resort and Mineral Spa, which bills itself as "Saskatchewan's best-kept secret," but somebody must have loose lips. More than 120,000 people a year visit this rural resort from around Saskatchewan, Canada and by international travellers who have discovered one of our favourite soaking spots.

The Manitou Spring's predecessor was the Chalet Pool, built in 1929 and destroyed by fire in 1983. Opened in 1988, Manitou Springs is a full-service resort hotel with a family restaurant and lounge. Massage and several other therapeutic services such as full-body mud wraps are offered in the funky spa.

Sure, you can find restaurant meals and spa services almost everywhere these days. But, in the middle of a frigid January, what hotel guests and day-trippers primarily flock here for is the heated version of the adjacent lake.

Soakers lounge in the resort's heated mineral pool, sectioned off to offer water temperatures that range from 34 to 38 degrees, and catch up with other winter-weary Saskatchewanians or develop new international friends. The golden-brown water, which looks like it leaked out of a whisky barrel, originates from Little Manitou; over 40,000 litres of water are pumped in, then warmed and circulated.

The village of Manitou Beach enjoyed its resort heyday in the 1920s. Thousands came to enjoy the lake's mineral waters and two heated mineral pools. It was the most popular summer resort on the Prairies and even rivalled Banff's Hot Springs. But the big draw was the water: you can easily float in the lake's naturally buoyant water and visitors have actually been photographed reading a newspaper at the same time.

Only three bodies of water in the world share a similar mineral content: Little Manitou, Karlovy Vary in the Czech Republic and Israel's Dead Sea. Of the three, Little Manitou Lake has the highest levels of sulphate and magnesium, both of which are linked to healthy skin.

Little Manitou Lake and Manitou Springs are an authentic grassroots experience where you emerge heavily coated with minerals. It's the Dead Sea, right in our own backyard.

Details: *Little Manitou Lake is only accessible during our warm months while the Manitou Springs Resort and Mineral Spa is open year-round. Aspiring hotel guests should secure reservations before visiting Manitou Springs due to high volume periods, especially during winter. 1-800-667-7672, manitousprings.ca*

87 Harmonic Getaway

There are usually two types of innkeepers: those hotels who offer downtown, urban locations where business people can easily meet up and shopaholics can avoid tired feet by accessing their favourite stores; the other type of innkeeper offers peace and quiet from the stress of the city and necessary time to commune with nature.

Former Torontonians Lorne and Lidia Paice were searching for a peaceful retreat and a more relaxed lifestyle. That's when they discovered a sprawling building for sale in Manitou Beach on a hillside overlooking "the healing waters" of Little Manitou Lake.

The Paices began renovations in 1997 on their harmonious, two-building guesthouse. Now restored to its present condition, Harmony House is a funky 12-room B&B and mini convention centre for those who want intimate accommodations.

Harmony House's guests usually arrive for a soak in the mineral-rich lake or the indoor mineral spa pools at nearby Manitou Springs, to kick up their heels at the historic Danceland, or to visit North America's first bird sanctuary nearby.

Built in 1918, this historical landmark began life as a YWCA then operated as a United Church summer camp, a restaurant and even a museum before being restored.

The wraparound decks and spacious grounds provide weary visitors a chance to relax in a quiet spot where they can look down towards Little Manitou Lake and view Saskatchewan's stunning sunsets.

When guests manage to pull themselves out of Harmony House's rooms (with hand-sewn duvets and antique furnishings), the spacious dining room is where the Paices serve their famous wholesome breakfast that includes saskatoon berry tea, if requested.

Details: *Harmony House is a smoke-free environment and because it's such a beautiful B&B, I'm willing to overlook the Paice's "no pets" policy. Harmony House Bed & Breakfast and Convention Centre at Manitou Beach, (306) 946-2707, harmonyhousesask.com*

Hived away in the humble hamlet of Meacham, the Dancing Sky Theatre (DST) is definitely our province's best home-grown dinner theatre experience.

Rural impresarios Angus and Louisa Ferguson started their unique project in 1993 just east of Saskatoon in a converted former Ukrainian hall. When the couple acquired the space, it needed a new roof yet this was the only building in the small hamlet that would serve as a suitable theatre venue. It now seats 100 dinner theatre-goers.

For Saskatchewan theatre buffs, DST's productions are considered a cultural must-see. Quirky Canadian-made productions like *Saltwater Moon, Mary's Wedding, The Red Truck* and *Farmer Joe and the Money Tree* have all graced their marquee.

The company's grassroots, hands-on philosophy (Angus is the artistic director and director and Louisa is the general manager and cook) has won them a loyal following and critical acclaim. In 2008, DST took home five out of 11 Saskatoon and Area Theatre Awards.

DST caters to a mainly rural, grassroots audience base but it also draws discerning urbanites from nearby Saskatoon. The Fergusons want to generate a genuine feeling of community as they offer customers a hearty meal followed by some great live theatre. The licensed dining space provides vegetarian options in addition to simple yet fresh fare like ribs and pasta.

The Dancing Sky Theatre is open on Friday and Saturday nights during winter and spring seasons (Sunday matinees are provided for seniors who don't want to drive at night) and closed during the summer.

Details: *Dancing Sky Theatre is located in Meacham, 67 kilometres east (40 minutes) of Saskatoon on Highway 2, south of Highway 5 and north of the Yellowhead Highway. (306) 376-4445, dancingskytheatre.com*

89   Red Teeth in Bruno

We've all eaten our annual quota of saskatoon berries. But have you sampled our very own regional red fruit, the dwarf sour cherry?

Since 2004, the town of Bruno near Humboldt has hosted the annual Bruno Cherry Festival. Attendees experience a few days of stained teeth, full stomachs and live music plus an appreciation of a hardy cherry that actually flourishes right here on the Prairies.

Over one late July weekend, the Bruno Cherry Festival traditionally features food delicacies (many featuring cherries, of course), a pancake breakfast, seminars, workshops, a small trade show, orchard tours, poetry, children's entertainment, a couple vintage car and motorcycle show 'n shines, a licensed lounge, live music entertainers and lots more.

The Bruno Cherry Festival celebrates the little red fruit on the grounds of the former Prairie Ursuline Centre, located along the northern perimeter of town. The centre was originally built as a convent in 1919 and when it became the St. Ursuline Academy in 1922, it earned a reputation for excellence in academics and cultural education over the next 75 years.

The University of Saskatchewan took over the facility in 1999 with the intention of running it as an extension-based conference facility.

The centre sits on an impressive 26 hectares, so in 2000 the university canvassed its research community to find out if anyone could make good use of the land. Dr. Bob Bors from the Department of Plant Sciences at the University of Saskatchewan decided this was a suitable spot for research plots to establish the dwarf sour cherry shrub.

The University of Saskatchewan bred the dwarf sour cherry specifically for the Prairies. These scrappy fruit trees possess exceptional cold hardiness, excellent flavour and they're suitable for both our fruit bowl and for commercial processing, mostly as canned pie filling. Within four years, dwarf sour cherry plants are well-established and producing fruit.

Over the next few years, the mature dwarf sour cherry shrubs, which grow to about two metres, eventually sparked the Cherry Festival in 2004. Bruce Hobin from the University of Saskatchewan's Extension Division, along with enthusiastic community volunteers, have created one of Saskatchewan's unique summer cultural events. But all Saskatchewanians know if a festival offers food, we're there in a heartbeat.

Although the university no longer holds the lease for the centre, the dwarf sour cherries continue to thrive on the property and the festival is organized every July with the support of the community.

Where else in Saskatchewan would you find a Saturday evening Cherry Festival Country Supper with cherries worked into the dishes, a Cherry Pit Spitting challenge or a Cherry Store to buy sour cherries, dried sour cherries, pies and even sour cherry shrubs to start your own orchard?

Details: *The Bruno Cherry Festival is held over one weekend in late July. Bruno is located 80 kilometres east of Saskatoon on Highway 5 (on the way to Humboldt). Follow the Bruno and Cherry Festival signs north for six kilometres. (306) 682-5936, cherryfestival.ca*

North

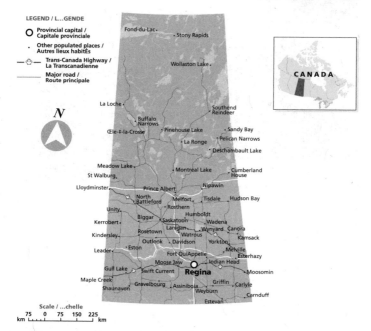

CANADA

Scale / Échelle
75   0   75   150   225
km └┴┴┴┘   └ km

---

91   Canada's Thoreau

What if the federal government offered you, your family and your pet beavers a free place to live in a beautiful new national park? Although you may start to resent being a sideshow spectacle for the curious tourists, you'd probably jump at the chance to work on that long-delayed adventure novel.

That's what happened to Canada's Thoreau.

Grey Owl was one of Canada's best-known environmentalists and a Native impersonator. Archibald "Archie" Belaney, an Englishman who arrived in Canada during the early 20th century when he was only 17, was a novelist and defender of Canada's wilderness. Belaney/Grey Owl travelled around North America and several times to Europe to promote conservation to the elites.

In 1931, Parks Canada wardens re-located Grey Owl, his Mohawk wife Anahareo and their two pet beavers, Jellyroll and Rawhide, from Manitoba's Riding Mountain National Park to the newly minted Prince Albert National Park.

Grey Owl's cabin, now a National Heritage Site and a lesser-known icon of Canadiana, stands discreetly in Saskatchewan's forested half

just a few hours north of Saskatoon on the edge of Ajawaan Lake. A trickle of visitors, mostly from North America and Europe, set off in sleek canoes every summer to discover the home of Canada's first conservationist.

This scenic trip starts from a take-in point on the meandering Kingsmere River, which links Waskesiu and Kingsmere lakes. After paddling to the north end of Kingsmere Lake, and a 15-minute portage to tiny Ajawaan Lake, it's only another 15-minute paddle to the cabin site. In good conditions, a group can canoe and portage to Grey Owl's cabin within five hours from the parking lot. Kingsmere's Northend campground features primitive sites and group camping.

The cabin site is appropriately sparse. Grey Owl's cabin contains a beaver lodge, located right inside the cabin, where the mating pair of Jellyroll and Rawhide eventually spawned Wakanee, Wakanoo, Silverbells and Buckshot. A log bed, a woodstove and a guestbook for comments from Grey Owl's most recent visitors round out the contents.

An upper cabin, built in 1932, housed his wife, Anahareo, their daughter and visitors, since apparently only Grey Owl enjoyed sleeping in the same room as busy beavers. Grey Owl, a.k.a. Archie Belaney, who died in 1938 at 49, is buried beside his wife and daughter near the upper cabin.

If the canoe route doesn't interest you, a 20-kilometre hiking trail adjacent to Kingsmere and Ajawaan lakes also accesses Grey Owl's cabin site. But if you want to follow in the path of Grey Owl's paddle, a canoe trip is still the best way to celebrate his eccentric legacy.

Details: *Before setting out to Grey Owl's cabin site, visitors must drop by the park office in Waskesiu to register and to purchase backcountry camping permits. 1-888-773-8888, pc.gc.ca; Waskesiu Marina Adventure Centre provides canoe rentals and guided trips; (306) 663-1999, waskesiumarina.com*

TAKE 5 GUY VANDERHAEGHE
A NOVELIST'S FIVE
HISTORICAL HAUNTS

Born in Esterhazy, author Guy Vanderhaeghe won the Governor-General's Award and the Faber Prize in the UK for his first book of short stories, *Man Descending* (1982). He has also penned several novels, *My Present Age* (1984), *Homesick* (1989) and *The Englishman's Boy* (1996), partially set in the Cypress Hills; Guy adapted his Governor-General Award-winning book into a two-part mini-series broadcast on CBC Television in 2008 and won six Geminis. His follow-up historical fiction novel, *The Last Crossing* (2002), was CBC Radio One's "Canada Reads" favourite in 2004. Guy lives in Saskatoon with his wife Margaret.

1. **Fort Walsh National Historic Site**. Located in one of Saskatchewan's most remarkable landscapes, the Cypress Hills, Fort Walsh and Abe Farwell's whisky post (which played a role in the Cypress Hills Massacre), are powerful evocations of life in the 1870s. Many of the West's most flamboyant characters are linked to this spot: James Walsh, Sitting Bull, Jerry Potts and Sam Steele, to name only a few.

2. **Wanuskewin Heritage Park**. Wanuskewin was central to the spiritual life of First Nations people for over 6,000 years. A great place to stroll, view a medicine wheel, buffalo rubbing stone and learn about First Nation's history and culture in a top-notch interpretive centre, just outside of Saskatoon.

3. **Batoche National Historic Site**. This is where Métis resistance to Ottawa was broken by Canadian troops. Rifle pits and bullets in a wall testify to the broken dreams of the Métis nation and their messianic leader, Louis Riel.

4. **Cannington Manor Provincial Historic Park**. Situated near Moosomin, the Manor tried to transplant Victorian England to the Prairies. The Beckton "boys" lived in a twenty-four-room mansion, fox hunted and were attended by valets. The wonky experiment ended in 1900.

5. **Kaposvar Historical Site.** In 1886, an immigration agent claiming to be Count Paul Esterhazy established a Hungarian settlement in the area. Using local stone, settlers built an impressive Catholic church with a grotto to the Virgin Mary a few kilometres south of Esterhazy.

Long before environmentalism became trendy, Forest House's founders, eco-pioneers Rick Kolstad and Deb Peters, built their four-seasons eco-lodge to be off the grid and off the beaten track. Using local materials, they generated power via solar panels, grew an organic garden and put in a self-composting septic system.

Forest House, Saskatchewan's premiere solar-powered, four-seasons eco-lodge, is located 150 kilometres north of Lac La Ronge on the shores of a small, pristine and unnamed lake in the McLennan Lake area.

Forest House was constructed to impose minimal impact on the delicate boreal forest eco-system. The main lodge, two cabins and mature organic garden have taken over 30 years to fully develop. Original builders Rick Kolstad and Deb Peters created their isolated vision with lumber harvested from the local forest then installed banks of solar collectors to generate power and a self-composting septic system.

Every detail of Forest House's construction, from location to materials to the self-sustaining garden, was planned to create a union between technology and the natural beauty of the boreal forest. The new owners, Ric Driediger and Thomas Marr-Laing, continue the original builders' vision in Saskatchewan's northern "Eden."

Lucky guests in these luxurious, eco-friendly accommodations enjoy gourmet meals sourced from terraced organic gardens, explore surrounding lakes with a small fleet of canoes and kayaks, hike the boreal forest, observe wildlife, check out pictographs, stargaze or slip in for a sauna beside the lake. Forest House isn't exactly roughing it in the northern woods, but why suffer when environmental technology can lend a hand?

Details: *Forest House is open year-round. Winter phone: 1-877-511-2726, Summer phone: (306) 635-2248, foresthouse.ca*

93 The Boreal Sahara

It might not get as hot or cover as large an area as the Sahara desert, but the Athabasca sand dunes certainly does resemble that North African region.

The Athabasca sand dunes aren't actually a desert. They're dune fields in the extreme northwest that stretch for roughly 100 kilometres along Lake Athabasca's southern shore. This anomalous surface is the largest active (still shifting) sand surface in Canada plus it's one of the most northerly set of major dune fields in the world.

An Athabasca Denesuline legend states that a giant beaver created the dunes. The Athabasca sand dunes were actually formed about 8,000 years ago during the last glacial period when the ice-sheet retreated from the area. While the glaciers might have moved on, the sand hasn't. The dunes gradually move according to the prevailing wind direction and this shifting sand slowly encroaches on the boreal forest.

Just as the Athabasca sand dunes offer bizarre scenery, it also offers a unique ecosystem. Scientists consider this isolated spot to be an evolutionary puzzle because it features 52 rare plant species that includes nine plant species unique only to this area.

To protect this sensitive environment, Athabasca Sand Dunes Provincial Wilderness Park was created in 1992. The park encompasses 1,925 square kilometres and it's been divided into three management zones; each zone has different guidelines to control camping and visitor activities.

Although you may fly in at considerable expense on a float plane — the only available access — don't even think about taking home souvenir plants, trees, ventifacts (rocks that have been abraded, pitted, etched, grooved, or polished by wind-driven sand or ice crystals) and artefacts — or face considerable fines. However, the fishing is top-notch and allowed.

Since there are no services, facilities or roads of any kind near or within the park, the Athabasca sand dunes are recommended for fully equipped, self-contained and experienced wilderness travellers.

In other words, enjoy the park, but you're on your own. And remember; don't take anything home but photos and memories.

Details: *Camping and campfires are permitted only in certain areas of the park; there are six designated primitive camping areas. Guided interpretative trips are also available to explore the dunes on foot or by boat. (306) 425-4234, tpcs.gov.sk.ca/AthabascaSandDunes*

If your most daring summer activity is drinking beer and barbequeing on your deck, here's a way to generate some adventures you can brag about to your friends, family and workmates.

Discover why *Kisiskatchewan* translates in Cree as "swift current"

TAKE 5   BUTCH AMUNDSON
AN ARCHAEOLOGIST'S FIVE FIELD-TESTED COUNTRY KITCHENS

Leslie "Butch" Amundson is the senior archaeologist with Stantec Consulting in Saskatoon. Butch lives in nearby Wakaw with his wife Debbie and daughter, SaraJayne; their older son, Kristofor, attends the U of S in Saskatoon. During 30 years of travelling off Saskatchewan's beaten paths, Butch has learned that much as an army marches on its stomach, an archaeology crew digs using the same organ. To prevent culinary mutinies, a varied menu at a lone rural restaurant is essential to crew morale. The following meet at least one requirement of the field archaeologist's rural eatery.

1. **Jack's Café in Eastend**. A breakfast of pancakes and sausage, bacon and eggs or fresh fruit with a perpetually full cup of strong coffee is a great way to start a day in south-western cattle country. One can choose a booth, a table or belly up to the counter and enjoy the depiction of frontier life in murals and artefacts that adorn the walls. Jack's is equal to the task of providing three squares. Their bagged roast beef on whole wheat is as good as any urban deli could prepare. In the evening, you can return for a Greek salad that's a meal unto itself or have a steak worthy of ranch country.

2. **Fife Lake Hotel in Fife Lake**. "The Best Steaks in Town" reads the road sign for the Fife Lake Hotel. Once you turn off Highway 18 and onto the main drag, you'll get the joke: they're the only steaks in town. Yet, after a shift at a coal mine, there's nothing like a barbequed steak and a cold beer to cap the day. Every night is "Steak Night" at the hotel, so while the crew gathers to relax in the steak pit, I grill the steaks to their specifications. Cole slaw, pickles and baked potatoes with all the fixins accompanies this Saskafeast and if the first beer tasted particularly good, maybe the field notes can wait for one more.

on the "Boreal Forest Primer" canoe trip. Operated by La Ronge-based Churchill River Canoe Outfitter, this eight-day, flora-meets-fauna, 150-kilometre adventure takes paddlers through a series of island-filled lakes — all joined by rapids or falls and 12 portages.

But it's not all about dodging rocks and waterfalls. Most paddlers spend considerable time watching eagles and pelicans during these magnificent birds' daily food hunt.

This gutsy canoe trip on the mighty Churchill River ferries paddlers

3. **Yang's Apollo Restaurant in Rocanville.** This Chinese restaurant, just down the street from the world's biggest oil can, is another three-meal eatery that makes it easy to pull duty in east-central Saskatchewan. Yang's offers a full breakfast menu and a range of deli lunch sandwiches that gets us through the day. But the real treat is supper when the crew each chooses a dish from the Chinese menu. The Apollo has arguably the best wonton soup, lemon chicken and chicken fried rice I've ever eaten. There's no problem getting the crew to sit down to the same meal every evening while we work in the region. But, if we do need a culinary break, a superb burger waits across the street at the Rocanville Hotel.

4. **Kosta's II Restaurant in La Ronge**. When work takes us to La Ronge, there's really only one place to go for supper. Catering to the sport fishing and mining crowd, Kosta's provides a great choice for the evening meal. I especially enjoy their baked lasagna and, in season, Lac La Ronge whitefish on a bed of locally harvested wild rice that provides a uniquely northern dining experience.

5. **Eddy's Roadhouse in Estevan**. After days — or weeks — of dropping drive-through gut bombs or eating in greasy spoons of questionable standards, Eddy's Roadhouse is a dining room in the southern oil patch where one can dine on pasta, French bread and a perfectly grilled steak — all chased down by a bottle of fine red wine. Though the elegant décor and fare would suggest otherwise, a dusty, sunburned crew of archaeologists decked out in sweaty old hats and army surplus clothes is more than welcome.

from Sandfly Lake to Otter Rapids and traces the path of the fur trade-era Voyageurs eastward into Manitoba. You get to hear adventurous stories about these pre-18-wheeler cargo shippers while you paddle by ancient rock paintings created by other early inhabitants.

The Churchill River, connected by a series of lakes joined by short rapids or waterfalls, flows over the Precambrian Shield, which is the western section of the rocky Canadian Shield.

In eight days, paddlers cover 105 kilometres and travel approximately 14 clicks per day, or about four hours of paddling. And just in case you're afraid of perching your canoe over your head for several kilometres at a time, there are only nine portages on the route that average 300 metres each.

Besides time spent communing with nature, ten percent of your trip fees are donated to the Canadian Parks and Wilderness Society (CPAWS), an environmental organization committed to protecting the Churchill River and preserving this incredible wilderness.

Details: *The Boreal Forest Primer pushes off in mid-August for eight days. At press time, the cost was $2,495/person with a $500 deposit required with your application. For a group of 5 or more, you can customize the dates and the content of this paddling program to suit your needs. 1-877-511-2726, churchillrivercanoe.com*

95   Chill Out at Ness Creek

Every third weekend in July since 1989, Saskatchewan's mysterious, elusive hippies surface for another chance to party in the northern woods.

Ness Creek's hippies gather around a few small stages that feature largely unknown artists from across Canada. If you join them, you can expect to hear roots music that ranges from Saskatchewan folk to world beat to blues to Americana country — all enjoyed by a mix of young and old, rural and urban.

The Ness Creek Cultural & Recreational Society is a not-for-profit organization that exists primarily to create an annual festival to celebrate music, arts, community and ecology in the boreal forest.

The Ness Creek Music Festival is based on a smaller event, the Ecological Fair, which was held in 1989 and 1990 near the current festival site northeast of Big River. The original gatherings featured ecological workshops, displays and a small evening stage with local musicians.

In 1991, the first Ness Creek Music Festival was held in its current location near the southwest corner of Prince Albert National Park. Once just a two-day festival with seven bands and 200 people has now grown into a four-day music and wilderness festival attended annually by 2,700 enthusiasts enjoying over 20 main stage performances.

This family-friendly event provides onsite camping with minimal services, concessions, children's activities, a craft market, an eco village and that popular spot to hang out with friends while the next band sets up, the beer gardens.

While the Ness Creek Festival continues to grow each year, the organizer's mandate is still to provide an audience for upcoming Saskatchewan artists by maintaining a minimum 50 percent ratio of Saskatchewan talent.

Details: *The Ness Creek Cultural & Recreational Society is a volunteer run organization. Learn more about being a volunteer or for tickets at the Ness Creek Music Festival: (306) 652-6377, nesscreek.com*

96   Meet Me at Waskahiganihk

Reverend James Nisbet's Presbyterian mission in Prince Albert (Saskatchewan's oldest city) dates to the mid-1860s yet there was a Hudson Bay Company's fur trade post at Cumberland House almost a century earlier.

Cumberland House, named for Prince Rupert, Duke of Cumberland, is the oldest continuously occupied site in Saskatchewan and the first western inland post built by the Hudson's Bay Company (HBC).

The post was established in 1774 by the HBC's Samuel Hearne as a supply centre to eradicate competition from independent traders — like an 18th century Walmart. HBC's competitors were intercepting furs from the area's Native people so the construction of Cumberland House meant HBC now expected Native people to bring their furs to

trade only at HBC posts.

The HBC's key reason for this isolated northern site was its established location on Pine Island in the Saskatchewan River delta, smack dab on the southern edge of the Canadian Shield, and a key route in the fur trade where boats could travel east to Hudson Bay via Lake Winnipeg or west to the Rocky Mountains. The Cree already called it Waskahiganihk and its island location meant it was a meeting place for area Native peoples.

Cumberland House is now a community of 800 inhabitants located 90 kilometres from The Pas, Manitoba. An all-weather road in 1967 finally connected Cumberland House to the south although this predominately Métis island community, adjacent to the Cumberland House Cree Nation, had to wait until 1996 for a bridge across the Saskatchewan River.

Cumberland House has been reduced to only a stonewalled 1890s-era powder house, used for storing gunpowder. The iron anchor and other pieces of the Northcote, a fur trade steamboat used at Batoche during the 1885 North West Rebellion, can also be viewed.

Since there are no camping facilities or any staff available at the park, visitors can start out from Nipawin or Carrot River for a day trip to Cumberland House Provincial Park. The site has been preserved merely for its historical significance and interpretive signs are in place.

Details: *Cumberland House Provincial Park can be accessed via 100 kilometres of gravel road on Highway 123. Saskatchewan Parks provides a brochure that describes the history of Cumberland House and the significance of the park. (306) 953-3571, tpcs.gov.sk.ca/CumberlandHouse*

97 Uranium Country Lodge

You've heard of a one horse town? Uranium City, Saskatchewan's most northern "city," is a one hotel town.

Located 724 kilometres northwest of Prince Albert and a mere 48 kilometres south of the Saskatchewan–Northwest Territories boundary, you hope Aurora Lodges doesn't put up the "No Vacancy" sign or else you'll be sleeping under the *aurora borealis*.

If you're travelling north to Uranium City, positioned on the northern shore of Lake Athabasca, you're probably not going there on a shopping holiday. Most of the businesses have taken down their shingles after the Beaverlodge uranium ore mine, run by Eldorado Mining and Refining Ltd., ceased operations in 1982.

Uranium ore was first discovered in northern Saskatchewan in the late 1930s yet the provincial government didn't start construction of this remote community until 1952 with the plan to provide infrastructure for 5,000 inhabitants.

By 1956, it was the fastest growing community in Saskatchewan then Uranium City almost died out by the early 1960s as the population rose and fell based on world uranium demand. In 1981, there were 2,500 residents and after Eldorado Nuclear shut down in 1982, the population had plummeted to 200 inhabitants by 1986.

Most people who now endure the long flight to Uranium City go to fish in Lake Athabasca, which covers 7,850 square kilometres and is the former home of the largest lake trout ever reeled in, a 46.3-kilogram whopper. This huge lake is also home to over 20 fish species plus the unique Lake Athabasca sand dunes are located near the lake's southern shore.

So, the Aurora Lodges these days is the only place to lay your head. But luckily it's a great place to stay. Whether you love to fly fish, cast or troll, the folks at the Aurora Lodges will recommend either area lakes or arrange fishing gear rentals, boats and local guides that know all the sweet spots.

Located in a secluded creek-side hideaway minutes from lakes, hiking, fishing and downtown Uranium City, Aurora Lodges' amenities range from northern four-star elegance to keepin' it real rustic outback cabins.

Big spenders can rent an entire lodge (accommodation, food, transportation, phone) and in certain cases, lodges are rented out on a "straight rental" where a group assumes full responsibility for essentials but it doesn't include staff or services.

Details: *Aurora Lodges are located beside Uranium City's historical Hospital Hill district. Rooms in the land of aurora borealis skies range from $125-$175/night per person. (306) 545-3994, auroralodges.com*

98	P.A.'s Cultural Hub

If your northern city of only 35,000 regularly plunges to a balmy –40 degrees, you better build a really stunning arts centre. Not only does it attract the locals, but those major touring acts that generally stick to big city venues will show up, too.

Prince Albert's E. A. Rawlinson Centre definitely sticks out. Opened on April 2, 2003, this attractive glass, metal and red brick facility houses both the John G. and Olive Diefenbaker Theatre and the Art Gallery of Prince Albert.

The E. A. Rawlinson Centre for the Arts is named for the late E. A. ("Ed") Rawlinson, a pioneer Canadian broadcaster, Prince Albert community leader and Founder of Rawlco Radio. A $1 million gift from Rawlco Radio was the seed money to create this visual and performing arts centre for central and northern Saskatchewan.

The Diefenbaker Theatre is possible because of a generous donation from the Diefenbaker Trust Fund for the theatre's operations budget. The theatre seats 612 — 402 on the main floor and another 210 in the balcony — considerably more seats than the parliamentary scrapping arena where The Chief spent a good portion of his political life when he wasn't in his Prince Albert home riding.

Whether it's performances by Saskatchewan talents Little Miss Higgins and Andrea Menard, other Canadian touring acts like Alex Cuba and comedian Ron James or large-scale productions like the Moscow Ballet's "The Great Russian Nutcracker," the E. A. Rawlinson Centre can compete on the same footing as Saskatoon's TCU Place or Regina's Conexus Arts Centre.

Located in the same facility, the Art Gallery of Prince Albert contains almost 600 art pieces in its permanent collection plus it features rotating exhibitions from regional artists, special events and outreach programming.

Details: *The E. A. Rawlinson Centre is located at 142 – 12th Street West north of Gateway Mall. (306) 765-1270 or 1-866-700-ARTS, earawlinsoncentre.ca; Art Gallery of Prince Albert, (306) 763-7080, artgalleryofprincealbert.com*

99   Big Pike in the Prize Pool

If he could have, irascible author and angling enthusiast Ernest Hemingway would have shown up for Nipawin's summer-long fishing contest.

Since 1969, the annual Nipawin Great Northern Pike Festival has attracted anglers from across North America to Tobin and Codette Lakes in hopes of catching one of 40 tagged northern pike and a prize pool of over $110,000.

All a participant needs for this catch-and-release contest is a valid angler's licence and a $5 entry fee. On average, 1,500–2,000 participants try their luck each summer while bobbing around on these two prize fish lakes. In 2008 alone, entries came from seven provinces and 16 states.

The Festival commences on Father's Day in June and continues until September 30. The elusive prize has been one $5,000 tag with a northern pike connected to it. The $5,000 tag was first caught in 1975 and over the years, additional major and grand prizes have been added.

So how does it work? The Great Northern Pike Festival hosts an annual Media Day on the first Monday in June where media personalities from across Saskatchewan descend on Nipawin to tag and release 40 northern pike in two separate lakes, Tobin and Codette.

Each tag has a number and they're placed in small separate envelopes. Four envelopes are drawn at random and they represent which tags will be the Pike Festival's major prizes. Then, in a sacred ritual, the remaining tags are burned inside a metal replica of a northern pike. If a tagged fish is caught, the tag is clipped off, the fish is live-released and the tag is returned to any official festival collection point on either Tobin or Codette Lake.

During this summer-long event, the town of Nipawin is adorned with colourful five-of-diamonds designs on Pike Festival banners plus every entry includes a $5 voucher for a local restaurant.

Detail: *Anglers can find out more info about registrations and prizes at (306) 862-7714, nipawin.com/pikefestival*

100   Volcano Highway

Some highways are so straight and boring you can literally set the cruise control on your RV and go put on the coffee pot.

Not the Hanson Lake Highway. In 1963, this much-needed highway opened a portion of Saskatchewan's vast north to forestry and mining. The 330-kilometre route takes adventurers through some of the most dramatic boreal forest landscape in Saskatchewan. It also provides evidence of two billion years of geological history, which ranges from limestone outcrops of an ancient seabed to the glacial remains of volcanoes.

Like many remote destinations in Saskatchewan, I suggest you enjoy the Hanson Lake Highway from spring to fall. Starting from the parkland forest city of Prince Albert on Highway 55, travellers drive northeast to Smeaton then turn north onto Highway 106 to start the Hanson Lake Highway.

Many are destined for Narrow Hills Provincial Park while others brave the entire route to Creighton near the Manitoba boundary — or onward to the adjacent, isolated mining community of Flin Flon, Manitoba.

The Narrow Hills, 150 kilometres from Prince Albert, are a sprawling, unique landscape, carved roughly 10,000 years ago by glacial ice sheets. This provincial park, too isolated for most urban weekenders, is known for great canoeing, camping, fishing, hiking, cycling and resort amenities such as a sandy beach at the Lower Fishing Lake's main campground.

The park's natural attractions include the Narrow Hills Esker, a substantial ridge of sand and gravel formed by a stream that once flowed under melting ice sheets. Make sure to take the Narrow Hills Scenic Drive where those glacial ice sheets left behind a substantial pile of hills, ridges and other majestic vistas you can spot from your vehicle's windows. For the self-propelled set, the Gem Lakes Hiking Trail features a spectacular view of a cluster of deep, sand-bottomed lakes that reflect a spectrum of aqua blue, jade and emerald illuminations. Who needs Lake Louise?

The next leg of the journey, from Narrow Hills Provincial Park to Creighton, is 250 kilometres. You'll find most resorts along the entire Hanson Lake Highway offer both lodging and camping facilities.

Visitors to the frontier town of Creighton can check out the area's gold rush history in the Creighton Museum & Tourism Centre, go on scenic drives, walking tours and explore ancient sea remains in the limestone crevices.

As you drive back south on this isolated yet very scenic route, repeat the same activities, which includes enjoying the stunning aurora borealis swirling overhead at your lodge or campsite.

Details: *Narrow Hills Provincial Park, accessible by Highway 106, is open year-round. (306) 426-2622 or 1-800-205-7070, tpcs.gov.sk.ca/NarrowHills; Creighton Museum & Tourism Centre, located at 216 Creighton Avenue, (306) 688-3538, townofcreighton.ca/Tourism.html*

101 Home of the Lobstick, the Pelican and the Vacationer

Prince Albert National Park's townsite, Waskesiu, is just like Banff's: surrounded by forest and lakes, lots of surly elk and filled with Parks Canada's trademark brown buildings. Of course, P.A. Park doesn't feature any mountains and, thankfully, even a large populace. The townsite of Waskesiu, which makes up less than one percent of the park area, experiences a noticeable annual population shift when it rotates from a winter low of less than 100 plucky souls to a summer average of 2,500 residents — not including campgrounds.

This unpretentious national park and townsite is a meeting place between the parkland and the northern boreal forest. It's also a gathering place for possibly half of Saskatchewan's summer vacationers and probably half of Alberta's — those former Saskatchewanians who return for a family getaway during our fleeting blast of summer heat.

You can wander this easily accessible park town, hang out at its white sand beaches beside Lake Waskesiu, rent a regular 16-footer or go big with a 25-foot Voyageur canoe at the Waskesiu Marina Adventure Centre. Classic family cottages can be found just down the road from rental units like Kapasiwin Bungalows and Armstrong Hillcrest Cabins that look right out of a 1950s summer getaway brochure.

Some people show up in Waskesiu just to participate in the annual Lobstick Invitational — a Saskatchewan summer tradition since 1935 — which attracts more than 700 golfers from across the continent to the four Lobstick tournaments.

Prince Albert National Park is rife with Saskatchewan tradition, heritage and before it was a recreational hotspot, this 3,875-square-kilometre park was exploited for its natural wealth. Luckily, on August 10, 1928, Prime Minister William Lyon Mackenzie King officially opened Prince Albert National Park to protect a mere section of our parkland and boreal forest.

This slice of protected land an hour north of Prince Albert features a bevy of natural wonders such as the only completely protected white pelican nesting colony in Canada and a free-range herd of reintroduced Plains bison. It also has its cultural treasures, including the cabin and burial place of conservationist Grey Owl. P.A. National Park offers over 1,500 lakes, sloughs and streams (which comprises 30 percent of the park), 180 kilometres of hiking trails, 500+ campsites at numerous campgrounds and kilometres of sandy beaches.

For those who need to shake a case of midwinter shackwacky, the park is also renowned for its 190 kilometres of cross-country ski trails.

Details: *Waskesiu/Prince Albert National Park is open year-round but with greatly reduced services during the winter. (306) 663-4519, parkscanada.ca; visit waskesiu.org for info on townsite services; canoe rental info at waskesiumarina.com*

Create Your Own

1.

2.

3.

4.

5.

Ultimate Must List

6.

7.

8.

9.

10.

Book of Everything Series

www.bookofeverything.com/bookstore.htm

Nova Scotia Book of Everything

New Brunswick Book of Everything

Newfoundland and Labrador Book of Everything

Prince Edward Island Book of Everything

Montreal Book of Everything

Ottawa Book of Everything

Toronto Book of Everything

Hamilton Book of Everything

Manitoba Book of Everything

Saskatchewan Book of Everything

Edmonton Book of Everything

Calgary Book of Everything

Vancouver Book of Everything

Vancouver Island Book of Everything

OVER 150,000 COPIES SOLD!

ENVIRONMENTAL BENEFITS STATEMENT

MacIntyre Purcell Publishing Inc saved the following resources by printing the pages of this book on chlorine free paper made with 30% post-consumer waste.

TREES	WATER	ENERGY	SOLID WASTE	GREENHOUSE GASES
9	3,100	6	399	750
FULLY GROWN	GALLONS	MILLION BTUs	POUNDS	POUNDS

Calculations based on research by Environmental Defense and the Paper Task Force.
Manufactured at Friesens Corporation